Whisperings of My Soul

*One Man's Journey from Husband & Father
to Amazing Grace and the Priesthood,
With Endless Grief, Eternal Love, & the Power of Prayer
Along the Way.*

ORLA
KELLY
PUBLISHING

Father Sean Hyland

Orla Kelly Publishing,
27 Kilbrody,
Mount Oval,
Rochestown,Cork

In Memory of My Darling Liz & Our Wonderful Children,
Seana & Kieran

Acknowledgements

In loving memory of my parents, Jack and Mary Hyland. Words cannot express my enormous sense of gratitude for their love and care and for all the sacrifices they endured to raise me.

My father, a quiet, hardworking, deeply selfless man will always be my hero. In my earliest years, I suffered from chronic asthma and bronchitis, and I have my mother to thank for her dedication in keeping me alive.

I try to carry with me their honesty, kindness and unwavering moral values.

I'd like to pay tribute to my sister Pat, who being a year older than me was my closest companion as a child.

In our later years, Pat experienced the loss of her husband and had the empathy to console and support me during my time of grief. Her gift of the verse *"Her Smile"* the week before she died is an enduring remembrance of her care for me.

Thanks to my sister May, through whom Liz communicates most of her messages to me. Through these heavenly blessings, you have given me priceless treasures, May.

And to my sister Kay for always being there and for constantly praying for me and my ministry.

I need to send special thanks to my brother P.J. and his wife Joyce - you always seem to know what I need before I even realise it myself. If ever I need to know what Liz would think about a situation or decision, all I have to do is ask you!

Dear Joyce, thank you for all your work collating lists of names and addresses and co-coordinating all the lists of the other family members for invitations to the ordination dinner. You organised the hotel, the menus, the seating arrangements etc. This was one area where I was most missing Liz, and you stepped in.

To all Liz's family, extended family and those who have joined me every year for the past nine years for Liz's anniversary mass.

Special thanks to Liz's sister Margaret who I know I'll see without fail every second Sunday at 3.00pm at Liz's grave. I'm grateful, Margaret, that you've maintained my link to all the rest of Liz's family.

To Niamh Broderick and Lorna Yates, our angels of mercy. You flew into Liz's and my lives and helped to make one of our worst times bearable. I thank God every day for sending you to us.

A special acknowledgement to my friend and former work colleague, Lionel Alexander. Thank you for having the belief, taking the trouble and having the courage to tell me that you received a message for me from Liz. Up to the time you phoned me in June 2009, my sister May had communicated a message she had received, and it seemed my brother P.J. had received some guidance from Liz regarding the gravestone. In moments of doubt during those first six months, I sometimes wondered if myself and my close family were so immersed in my grief that somehow we were emotionally or psychologically creating these events. Your calm, detached and objective communication left me in no doubt that these communications from Liz were very real. It allowed me to embrace these heavenly messages in a more fulsome and heartfelt way.

To Liz's dearest friends Dolores O'Shea, Mairead Arthur, Ann Cribben and Eileen Foley: You were always there for Liz, and now you're here for me.

Much gratitude to Eileen Ryan and Rosemary Whelan in the Portarlington parish office for all your hard work for my ordination - and the production of that mini-Book of Kells!

To Raymond Muldowney, my cousin and godson: Huge thanks for the gift of beautiful arrangements of red, white and gold roses on the altar to mark my ordination on the feast day of Our Lady of the Mystical Rose.

A double thanks to you and Carmel for the precious gift of the statue of Our Lady of the Mystical Rose. It now has pride of place in my prayer room.

Thanks to Doctor Fullam as our family doctor and as leader of that magnificent choir who performed at my ordination.

To the wonderful Julia Leavy and Marie Corcoran and all the parish social committee members who made the night of my mass of thanksgiving such a memorable occasion.

Thanks to Noel Healy for introducing me to the inspirational Father Fred MacDonnell.

To Father Paddy Byrne, you were the first person that I shared my writings with. I'm profoundly grateful to you for encouraging me to publish these lovely heavenly blessings at this time, rather than wait until I retired. You could not have been more supportive and encouraging all along. I'm doubly grateful, Father Paddy, for your suggestion to include a chapter on prayer.

To the diocesan vocations director, Father Ruairi O'Domhnaill, for having the courage to recommend a profoundly grieving 63-year-old as a candidate for the priesthood.

Thank you for being a companion and loyal supporter during my years at the Beda.

You were the second person I asked to review my early writings and help me decide if I should publish. You and P.J. convinced me to include most of the personal details of my life with Liz and my memories of Seana and Kieran.

Thanks too to Bishop Emeritus of Kildare & Leighlin, Jim Moriarty, for accepting Father Ruairi's recommendation and for all your support in my vocational discernment.

Grateful thanks to Father Joe McDonald and Father Paul Dempsey, members of the diocesan vocations discernment panel, for all your kindnesses too.

I want to express gratitude to Monsignor Rod Strange, for your calm and reassuring presence at the Beda. You ensured all at the Beda adhered to the highest standards of conduct, but you also cared for the welfare and formation of the seminarians.

To all the staff and the professors in that close-knit community in the Beda for your support and encouragement.

To all my fellow seminarians, and in particular my classmates at the Beda. We really were a band of brothers.

I'd like to acknowledge all the priests who have supported me through my discernment, my studies at the Beda and especially all the priests of Kildare and Leighlin Diocese who continue to mentor and support me in my ministry.

I know I can call on any one of you for support at any time. I have another band of brothers.

To Father Alex Kochatt from India, who arrived in Ireland in 2014 and who was assigned to Askea parish a few months before me; We spent a lovely year together: you teaching me the practical rudiments of priesthood; and I teaching you a little about Irish culture.

I've been fortunate to gain so much guidance in ministry from a series of parish priests during my discernment, my pastoral placements and in my ministry since ordination.

I've enormous regard and respect for these men, who have given their whole lives in the service of God and continue to dedicate their lives to the service and support of God's people.

I've worked in a demanding environment in the business and corporate world. Yet I constantly admire these men who manage to juggle spiritual, pastoral and counselling duties with entrepreneurial, managerial and financial ones every day.

I'm a late-comer to the priesthood and a curate, so I don't have to shoulder all those challenging responsibilities, but I think we should acknowledge all those men who do.

To Father Tom Little, my parish priest for my three years in Askea, Bennekerry and Tinryland. You are one of the most supportive and caring people I've had the privilege of meeting in my life.

And to Father Tom Dooley, parish priest of Portarlington, for believing in me and supporting me when I most needed it.

To Father Greg Corcoran, Father Larry Malone, Deacon Gary Moore and all the sacristans in Rhode and Clonbullogue for all your support.

I want to add my special thanks to the parish teams and the people of Askea, Bennekerry and Tinryland who wholeheartedly welcomed and encouraged me during my first three years of priesthood.

Also to the parishioners of Rhode and Clonbullogue parishes - thank you for welcoming me home and for showing your support for me every day.

To Kathryn, my editor, who with infinite patience has done a marvellous job turning my rambling dissertations into a finely crafted account of my heavenly blessings.

Thanks, in particular for extracting all the personal details of my life with Liz and the lovely memories of Seana and Kieran and weaving them into such a beautiful tapestry.

To Orla, my publisher, for guiding and supporting me on getting this book published and for educating me along the way on the importance of titles, subtitles and book covers.

Finally, much gratitude to Bishop Denis Nulty who not only ordained me to the priesthood but assigned me to the wonderful parishes of Rhode/Clonbullogue.

Thank you so much too for generously agreeing to preside at the launch of this book.

Contents

Contents Cont.

PART ONE

WHISPERINGS OF MY SOUL

"Be joyful always; pray continually; give thanks in all circumstances,
for this is God's will for you in Christ Jesus."
1 Thessalonians 5:16-18

Introduction

When I reached the lowest ebb of my life, I called out to God and discovered that He was there for me.

During a time of devastating loss and grief, He granted me gifts of incredible and beautiful consolations of faith.

I believe that these consolations of faith have been sent to me as assurances of God's love and mercy.

And that these gifts are also gentle reminders that - to my joy - my loved ones are aware of my everyday events and are watching over me too.

Saint Paul says God's love conquers all, even death.

And Saint John says: *"Whoever believes in Him shall not perish but have eternal life."* John 3:16.

Since the consolations of faith that I've experienced through my wife and children, I have no doubt about eternal life.

Somehow, through God's Grace, my family have been allowed to reach me and let me know they're close to me, so neither have I any doubt about eternal love.

And it's all about love. Everything, our journey on earth, this entire world, is all about love.

I've always believed that the divine gifts I received are not intended for my consolation alone. I've tried to share them with all those who need them and are open to receiving them.

And my fervent hope in writing this book is that my words reach other troubled people who need the love and support of Jesus and his Blessed Mother.

I want people to know how close they are and how they will comfort anyone who asks for help.

I also want people to know our loved ones in heaven are close to us too. I believe that they care about us, watch over us and constantly intercede with God the Father on our behalves.

I first started to write about all the consolations I received when I was studying in Rome. Until then, I had only shared them verbally with my family, Liz's family and some close friends.

Since being ordained, I share these experiences with anyone who I believe they can help. I am encouraged by the very positive response I get whenever I share them with people.

But I didn't plan to do anything further with my manuscript until my retirement.

Then in November 2017, Father Paddy Byrne launched his book, 'All Will Be Well'.

After reading it, I shared my experiences with Father Paddy, who encouraged me to work on publishing now, rather than when I retired.

I asked diocesan vocations director, Father Ruairi O Domhnaill to help me discern if I should publish these experiences while being a serving priest.

When I met with Fr Ruairi, I tried to describe to him how sensitive and precious these consolations are to me. The phrase that came to me was that they are 'the whisperings of my soul'.

Once I decided to publish these experiences, I became conscious of other material that I'd filed both on my computer and in my mind.

That material, concerning other greater manifestations of God, kept reminding me that it was there and that it didn't want to be left out.

I realise that my small consolations of faith are just that: modest, personal and very beautiful gifts from God. They now constitute part 1 of this book.

But I felt driven to write about the many other times when God reveals Himself in greater ways.

In particular, I wanted to write about three miracles that constantly resonate with me.

These are miracles which are irrefutable evidence of God's revelation in this world.

These three miracles and the fascinating results of scientific investigation into each of them now form Part 2 of this book.

I also wanted to look at other forms of God's revelation all over the world.

I've looked at how all empirical data and scientific evidence proves that belief in God is universal and growing. Yet, there is this strange consensus and myth that religion is in decline.

Part 3 of this book shows how the vast majority of human beings, at all times, all over the world, are believers.

Also, I wanted to explore the advances in science which are providing the greatest evidence for God's existence.

Part 3 shows that despite the rising tide of secularism all over the world, God is being revealed through modern science.

It seems to me from the outset that I have been writing only what I was inspired and guided to do. The wonderful consolations I received are a platform to communicate the other greater manifestations of God in the world.

As a result, this book is written in thanksgiving to God for His love and mercy. It's also written in the hope that my testimony can inspire others to become more open to His light and majesty.

They say miracles happen every day, and I know that to be true, because looking at my life today, I am that miracle.

And I'd love other lives to be as enriched as much as mine has since I began listening to the Whisperings of my Soul.

Sean Hyland

1

Love, Life & Liz

"You have captivated my heart with one glance of your eyes."
Song of Solomon 4:9

The first time I laid eyes on the love of my life was in the Dreamland ballroom in Athy in Kildare.

It was 1966, and I was a 19-year-old apprentice electrician from Portarlington in Laois, a half-hour's drive from the venue.

The Dreamland was one of a series of ballrooms owned by entrepreneurial Longford brothers, Jim and Albert Reynolds.

Inside, it was like a scene from the movie, The Ballroom of Romance, with the boys on one side of the room and the girls gathered on the other.

I'd travelled by hired hackney car to the dance with a group of friends from my hometown. We tried our best to look cool as we surreptitiously eyed the girls across the smoke-filled hall.

I saw Liz within minutes after my arrival and was captivated straight away.

Even from a distance, I could see there was something intense and beautiful about her eyes. When she smiled, I thought she lit up the room.

She was the only woman in the hall I wanted to dance with.

I don't remember who was playing that night, but as soon as the music started, I joined that mob of eager suitors dashing across the floor.

I locked eyes with her startlingly blue ones, and she gave me a shy smile.

Then my friend stepped in front of me a split-second before I reached her.

"Would you like to dance?" I heard him say even as the same words formed on my lips.

I hadn't realised that he had spotted her too.

She glanced at me apologetically as she headed to the dance floor with my friend.

I stood there awkwardly for a few seconds before gathering my wits and asking her friend to dance instead.

My heart sank further when the music stopped, and my friend invited the girl of my dreams to the bar for a soft drink or 'a mineral' as they were known then. He was interested in her.

I thought: *"Well, that's it, then."* He'd walk her home, and I'd never be able to ask her out.

I finished the dance with her friend but didn't invite her for a mineral. There was only one woman in the hall for me that night.

I was relieved when my friend appeared to share the hackney home with us that night. He said he couldn't walk her home that night because she'd arranged a lift with her brother.

The blue-eyed girl and I never exchanged a single word; I didn't even know her name, but I didn't forget her.

A few weeks later, I went to the former Crofton Hotel in Carlow where the local rugby club held their dances.

There was the girl with the piercing blue eyes again, and my heart started beating faster.

This time I made sure I was first across the floor to ask her to dance. She smiled a warm, wide smile of recognition as I approached.

Her name was Liz Myron, and she was the same age as I was. From the village of Arles in Laois, she lived about 50-minutes' drive from my home in Portarlington.

She was my first serious girlfriend, and I was her first real relationship.

And we were together after that night until she died over forty years later.

Wanting to spend as much time with her as possible, I got my best friend, Mick Corcoran, to teach me how to drive my father's Morris Minor.

I'd load up some of the lads and pick up Liz, and we'd go to the dances or to hear The Dubliners or some other band play in Naas.

Then the guys all found their own girlfriends and drifted away, and it was just me using the car to see Liz.

We were incredibly close from the beginning. Liz never played any mind games, and there was nothing ever confusing about our relationship.

From the very start, Liz let me know that I was the love of her life.

The first day to our last, I was never, ever left in doubt that she loved me more than anything.

She was the love of mine too, but I didn't express it for a long time. I wasn't an expressive man then, but I wish I had been.

There was never any doubt about us getting married either.

I finished my apprenticeship in 1969, and we got engaged and decided to go to Canada. There were good job opportunities there, and we wanted to see the world and save some dollars before we settled down.

We agreed that the move was for two years, and then we'd return to get married.

I worked as an electrician on the construction of a nuclear power plant outside of Toronto. Liz worked as a medical secretary with The Catholic Children's Aid Society.

We both loved Canada, the climate, the culture and the money we earned. We travelled to Niagara Falls, New York and many other places.

We returned to Ireland to get married as we had agreed. The wedding took place in Liz's home village of Arles on Saturday, February 12, 1972.

All her life, Liz had a great sense of style and her own distinct look. She rewrote the rules of fashion to suit herself, and her unique style came to the fore on the day she married me.

Her winter-wonderland themed wedding gown complete with a fur-trimmed hood and sleeves stood out in rural Ireland in those days.

Liz and I settled down in my hometown of Portarlington where we built our first house on my father's land.

We were different people in a lot of ways. I was impatient and a minor depressive who always saw the dark side of things. If anything went wrong, I was inclined to grumble, complain and kick up a fuss. Anything would set me off.

"We've come all this way for the sun, and it's raining! What kind of holiday is this? What are we supposed to do now?"

Liz was always inclined to see the bright side of everything and would always have a plan B.

"I'm glad it's raining!" she'd reply. *"It's the perfect opportunity to visit the art gallery and the museum. And we'd never have gone if it was sunny, would we?"*

Even when far bigger calamities struck, Liz had a mantra which put everything in perspective.

"Once we have one another, we can deal with whatever life throws at us," she'd say.

And even if we had a disagreement, or she was in a bad mood with me over something, there was never a doubt that she loved me with all her heart.

She always made it clear that I was the centre of her life. She was incredible because she made sure that there was never, ever a shadow of a doubt about that.

She showered me with love, affection and care, and I loved her too with all my heart. I could never get enough of her long elegant eyelashes and those bright sapphire blue eyes.

Her eyes darkened when she gazed into my eyes or her children's, as her pupils grew immense with love. She was beautiful mentally, physically and spiritually, and we were happiest when we were together.

I travelled a lot for most of my jobs, which we both found difficult. We never liked being apart from one another.

For one of my birthdays, Liz framed the sentiments below, and it still hangs in my hall today. The words hold so much meaning to me.

Just for You

When we are together
And no words are spoken
Love fills the silence

When we are apart
And not with one another
Love fills the distance

Whether we are together
Or whether we are apart
Love for you fills my heart.

"Love fills the distance…" Those words have even more meaning for me today. Because I know that whatever eternity is in terms of distance and time, Liz has been allowed by Jesus to bridge it on occasions.

She has been able to let me know in no uncertain terms that she's still with me. I know for sure that she's not far away.

She went out of her way to find messages and cards to let me know how much she loved me.

She'd spend hours looking for the one with the right sentiments. I still have another romantic verse from her that means a lot to me:

"I've often thanked my lucky stars
For matching me to you
My wonderful loving Hubby
Special in all you do.

As we've travelled life together
What happy times we've spent
A marriage made in heaven
A partnership truly meant

My heart still misses a beat
As only you can make it do
My soul mate and my sweetheart
I love you through and through."

Yet, much as I knew she loved me, I was always aware that I had to share her with her other great love - her faith.

I grew up in a very traditional Catholic home. I stayed going to mass every week in deference to my parents, but I didn't get much out of it.

As apprentice electricians, we had to spend three months every year studying at Kevin Street College of Technology in Dublin. It didn't bother me then not to go to Mass.

I shared digs with Sean Nugent, Eamonn O'Connell, Chris Daly and Liam Shanahan. We were all 17-year-olds up in the big city for the first time.

They claim I introduced them to smoking, drinking, fast women and slow horses.

They also say they've seldom seen a leopard change his spots so fast when I introduced them to Liz two years later.

In those days, I was drawn to socialism and the much more left-wing Labour Party of that era. I had the Che Guevara T-shirt; I read Karl Marx and Lenin.

I wasn't a communist by any stretch of the imagination, but I fancied myself as a bit of an intellectual.

Then I went to Canada, where I was transformed from a mini-socialist to a mini-capitalist.

I was always interested in learning, so I read up on world religions, but I wasn't what you'd call religious at all.

When I met Liz, we went to Mass, and there was no argument. There wasn't any question about it.

Her faith kept me connected to the church and inspired me to keep going, but I didn't get a lot out of it.

Her faith sometimes even irritated me. We liked to travel to exotic countries, and we went to many fascinating places like Cuba, China, Russia and Tokyo.

But as soon as we'd arrive in any foreign country, the first thing Liz would do is search for the nearest Catholic church. And this could be a challenge in countries like Cuba, China, Russia and Tokyo.

And it wasn't enough to be told where the church was. We'd have to go on a recce there on our first morning.

She had to make sure we knew exactly where it was; how long it would take to walk, or if we'd need to order a taxi for Sunday.

I often silently fumed. We went on some expensive holidays, and I resented spending the first half day searching for the location of the nearest church.

As I said, my anger was silent. I never voiced my frustration about this routine on every holiday. I learnt not to question it.

Liz did everything to support me, and she would have done anything for me, but mass was not even up for discussion.

She was quiet about her faith, but it was as much a part of her as breathing.

Anyway, after that first morning, we'd do whatever I wanted to do for the rest of the holiday.

But finding where we'd get Sunday Mass was a priority. I realised that's what we do.

A year after we married, the two of us became three with the arrival of a beautiful daughter. We couldn't have been happier with our perfect baby.

Liz being the diplomat she was, called her Margaret Mary Seana Hyland. Her mother and sister's name was Margaret, and she had another sister Mary which was also my mother's name.

But Liz said that our first child's given name would be Seana after me.

It was another thing that wasn't up for discussion. Liz decided it, and that was that.

Then in 1975, when Seana was two years old, she was taken to heaven. It shattered us, but Liz was a tower of strength. She kept me going in that awful first year.

A year later, we felt some hope and light in our lives again when Liz gave birth to our lovely son Kieran. But our little boy lived an even shorter life than his sister, and he died at ten-months-old in 1977.

I'll relate all about our beautiful children in a chapter dedicated to each of them.

We went to see consultants afterwards because we wondered about having more children.

As far as the medical opinion was concerned, Seana and Kieran's deaths were unrelated. They told us it was bad luck. They were one-in-ten-million kind of tragedies.

Having lost Seana, we were very anxious parents anyway. Every night there was one of us awake keeping an eye on Kieran.

Yet, we couldn't save him either.

We were afraid we wouldn't be able to cope with the anxiety, worry and heartbreak again. We couldn't deal with that gaping hole and terrible loss in our lives.

We agonised about it, and we prayed and then decided that we wouldn't have any more children.

We were 29-years-old and having once been parents to two children, we found ourselves childless. It was just Liz and me again.

But Liz was resolute.

"Once we have one another, we can deal with whatever life throws at us," she said again and again.

Our wedding day, Arles Church, February 12, 1972

2

Grief & Fury

"Be not quick in your spirit to become angry,
for anger lodges in the bosom of fools."
Ecclesiastes 7:9

After the children died, I was dark, questioning and angry. I raged about how God could do this to us, not once but twice. I was furious with God and with life in general.

Liz bore the loss with grace and a sense of serenity that I couldn't understand. She not only had to deal with her own grief, but she had to carry me as well.

After our little girl died, I put one foot in front of the other and kept going. There was still some hope for other children at that stage, even though I knew nothing could ever replace Seana in our hearts.

Seana had a big playpen which she used to pull herself into a standing position, and from there she commanded the entire household.

She had lots of toys including her favourite little tricycle. She often sat perched on her trike, in the corner of the kitchen, observing everything that Liz was doing.

When she died, we packed everything she owned into the big playpen, put it in a spare room and locked it up out of sight.

When Kieran was born, we took out Seana's toys again. We added to the vast collection of playthings by buying more toys including his lovely rocking horse.

The toys weren't out of storage for very long before Kieran left our lives too.

The day after Kieran's funeral, Liz packed all the toys into the big playpen, and we stored everything away again.

When we made the decision not to have any more children, Liz did the practical thing.

"I'm going to call the Gay Byrne radio show and ask them to collect the toys," she said. *"At least they'll do some good if they go to some needy children."*

Gay Byrnes's radio show had a charity collection of toys at the time, and they said they'd send someone with a trailer the next day.

I had mixed feelings over giving the toys away, but I didn't argue with Liz. I didn't have the heart or the energy.

Yet, I'll never forget seeing that trailer pulling away from the house.

As we watched Seana and Kieran's toys leaving our lives, the realisation hit us all over again that our children were gone and were never coming back.

Our lives had changed forever, and we'd never be parents again.

I railed against the injustice of losing our children, but Liz endured the loss with stoicism.

She never questioned; she never raged '*Why us?*'. She never fumed like I did. She remained her gentle, loving self.

Yet the loss for her must have been unbearable because she was the best mother imaginable.

Her great friend Dolores O'Shea said she remembered watching Liz and Seana together. She said she saw the bond and that love that flowed between them, and she said she envied Liz.

Dolores had her own lovely girl who she loves dearly, but even she recognised the unique connection they shared.

Yet Liz's faith was rock solid. It kept her going. She knew where her children were, and she never doubted it.

Liz knew she was going to be reunited with them in time. And in the meantime, she was going to take care of me. It was as simple as that.

She never wavered in that, and I never heard her complain once about the unfairness of it all.

When I say Liz was stoic, I don't mean she was grim and unemotional, accepting everything that life threw at her. She wasn't like that at all. Liz and was born with a cheerful disposition, and she loved to laugh.

She had a smile that sparkled in her incredible eyes. To me, she was like a light turning on in a dark room.

Everywhere became a better place when she smiled, and she smiled a lot. As I said, she looked on the bright side of life all the time.

She refused to entertain negative emotion. I never heard her talk in anger, or fear or jealousy, whereas I wallowed in negativity for a long time.

She couldn't stand any kind of gossip or rumours or any negativity about people. If we were out socialising and people around her were exchanging gossip, she tried to change the subject.

If she couldn't change the subject, then she'd make some excuse to leave. She'd get up to admire some flowers in a vase or to take a walk around the garden.

She couldn't bear unkindness in people.

Liz had already experienced tragedy by the time I met her in that dance hall in Athy in 1966.

Her older sister Mary was the pride of the family when she joined the Sisters of Mercy order.

As a novice nun, the order sent her to a Mercy convent school in Sheffield.

She was working in the school 'wash house', as they called it, when her habit caught fire. Sister Mary Clare Myron was only 21-years-old when she died of her injuries in hospital on Christmas Eve, 1963.

Liz's father wasn't well at the time, so her mother had to go to England to identify the body.

Liz's mother was the type of woman who always wanted to talk about Mary's death. She tried to tell everyone about her late daughter. It was her way of dealing with her grief.

Liz never seemed to like this. She never said anything, but I saw her try and change the subject whenever her mother talked about Mary.

Perhaps, Liz didn't want to be like her mother, or she didn't want anyone to feel sorry for her. She didn't want sympathy or to be a victim, and she didn't want to impose her grief on anyone else.

She steeled herself against the pain and faced the world with her own quiet dignity.

Liz endured more family heartache when her dad passed shortly after Seana died.

She also shared her older brother Jim's fears for his youngest child David.

David was a delicate child who had kidney problems from a young age. As a teenager, the problem got worse, and he was in and out of Our Lady's Children's Hospital in Crumlin for a long time having dialysis.

Liz and I lived in Dublin at that time, so she visited her nephew a lot, and she was very close to him

One day, Liz came home from the hospital, and she said David was getting worse, and it sounded like he might need a kidney transplant.

"Just to let you know, if he does need the transplant, I'd like to donate one of my kidneys," she said.

I was horrified at the idea, to be honest, but I knew there was nothing I could do about it.

"If that's what you want to do, Liz, I can't stop you," I said, but I secretly hoped that I could.

It was ironic that years later, it was kidney problems which ended Liz's life.

It turned out that David improved as he grew older, his kidneys recovered, and he didn't need the transplant. Everyone heaved a sigh of relief, especially me.

At last David could move on from his health problems and get on with his life.

Then one morning he was driving into DIT in Carlow when he skidded on a patch of oil and crashed into a truck.

His dad, Jim, heard about the accident minutes later on local radio. He knew the crash was down the road.

He raced down and was second on the scene, but David was already dead.

Jim died a couple of years afterwards, and everyone said it was of a broken heart.

Then Liz's mother died.

Liz was surrounded by grief and death, and yet I never heard her complain about the unfairness of it all.

We sold our home in Portarlington after the children died and moved to Dublin. It was too hard for Liz to live in our old house. She was surrounded by too many memories.

But we returned to visit the children in St Michael's Cemetery in Portarlington every Saturday at 3pm. You could set your watch by us.

We sometimes found it difficult at social gatherings when people asked the inevitable question *Do you have children?*

We were never going to deny our children, but when we said we have two children in heaven, it was a conversation killer.

No one knew what to say next.

I knew it was very hard on Liz, and it was one of the few situations where I tried to answer on her behalf.

When Liz moved to Dublin with me, she had to make a whole new circle of friends none of whom knew her background.

Liz's close friends told me she had a scripted reply anytime she was asked.

"I have two children in heaven. Our little girl Seana went to heaven when she was two-years-old and our little boy Kieran was one-year-old. I'd rather not talk about it anymore, if you don't mind."

Her friends respected her wish, so they never asked further.

They were always aware of how close Liz and I were, and she always made it clear that our relationship was precious to her.

She loved it too when she saw how much she meant to me. Like I said, I didn't always express how much I needed and loved her.

When I worked at Hewlett Packard, the staff grew from a few hundred people to a few thousand.

I needed to engage with a lot of these people, so I hosted a lunch in the cafeteria once a week for staff on a rotating basis.

Without even thinking about it, I'd bring Liz's name into these meetings where we threw around ideas.

I'd say things like: *"I'm trying to think what Liz would think of this"* and *"that's not how Liz would approach this."*

As soon as I introduced Liz at social gatherings at work, people would say: *"Great to meet you, at last, Liz! Sure we know all about you because Sean never stops talking about you."*

I remember how happy that made her. It seems like a little thing, but Liz treasured those remarks. It was a great source of joy to her to realise that I spoke about her so much.

We only ever had three Christmases with our children: two years with Seana and one with Kieran.

Liz never put up a Christmas tree after that, nor a decoration. Nor did she ever buy a Christmas card again. We went away that week every year instead.

In the early years we went to hotels in Ireland, and then we went abroad, usually to the Algarve.

We talked about the golf and the sun, and some people joked about our jet-set lifestyle, but we just wanted to get away on our own at Christmas.

There were too many reminders of what might have been. It's a time for children, and ours were gone.

Christmas Eve mass was the only part we celebrated, and then we got on with golf.

We enjoyed it, and it broke up the winter. But it was really about escaping all those reminders of Christmas past.

We'd get back for New Year's Eve to celebrate with her family and mine, but there was always something about Christmas that Liz couldn't handle.

Liz never worked outside the home after the children died. She didn't want to.

She was a tremendous housewife and loved looking after the home and taking care of me. I was on a high tax rate anyway, so there was little advantage in her working outside the house.

Instead, Liz took it upon herself to do everything at home. She handled the entire business of the house from cutting the grass to paying all the bills.

I never knew what was in our bank accounts, she looked after that. We'd go driving, and Liz would insist on driving.

She waved me off to work every day, but she handled everything after that. She wanted to do it, and I understood why.

She saw it as her job. That was her side of the deal. I'd always offer to help out, but she didn't like me getting involved in her side of things.

The way she saw it, she had her job, and I had mine.

For a long time, I didn't understand how Liz was so accepting about the loss of our children.

I always went to Mass every Sunday, but it was more for Liz's sake than my own. I was angry with God.

Yet, whenever when I got to my lowest ebb and tried to close the door on God, I always got a sense that the Virgin Mary was there watching over me.

Maybe I was hearing the whisperings of my soul even then, but all I know is that I couldn't deny the existence of God altogether.

I tried to draw what support I could from my faith, but it wasn't much.

I read a lot of science and philosophy books after the children died. I wanted to know where my children were.

I decided I would figure out how the world worked even if it involved wading through quantum physics books.

I borrowed three books from the library every week. One was on science or cosmology, one on philosophy, and one on religion.

I read all three at the same time because I didn't want to end up trapped in some kind of fundamentalist cul-de-sac. I wanted to explore as many ideas as possible.

I wanted to find my children. Did they exist anymore, I wondered? What possible purpose could their deaths achieve?

All around me felt like chaos. It was so random. Our babies were here one minute and gone the next.

"Is that it?" I asked. *"How can that be it?"*

Were Seana and Kieran in heaven as the Bible and Jesus promised? I wished I knew, but I didn't have Liz's conviction that they were safe.

I kept going to work as usual. At that stage, I was working for American manufacturing companies. We had lost our children, but I didn't want us to lose our home and hit skid row into the bargain.

But like I said, I was an angry man. The lads at work tried to do their best to raise my spirits afterwards. I warned them that I didn't want to talk about anything. Not sport, not money, not the weather.

"There's nothing in this world worth talking about, leave me alone," I said.

They left me alone. They knew to let me be. That continued for months after Kieran died. I spent my time pouring over these books and desperately hoping to find the answers that I was looking for.

In the years that followed I focused on my career to distract myself. I channelled a lot of my anger into aggression, ambition and assertiveness at work.

The one positive thing about that inner rage was that it turbo-fuelled my career.

Even though I must have been difficult to live with, Liz showed endless patience. The worse I got, the more unconditional love she gave me. She was always caring, understanding and supportive.

In a lot of ways, Liz reminded me of my father, a man I admired more than any other man.

Jack Hyland was another stoic person of faith who never complained or grumbled about anything.

Dad was hugely conscientious about his work, and he did it all with cheer.

He was a linesman with the ESB; he was a part-time fireman, and he had about 10 acres of land to work.

During Lent, he'd get up to milk the cows, work the farm, and then he'd attend daily mass before he spent a full day labouring for the ESB.

He did more work than a guy with a hundred acres because he had no machinery, and he did everything by hand.

Along with many small farmers in those days, he made ends meet by growing sugar beet under contract for the sugar factory in Carlow.

With this contract, you had a date when the wagons were at the railway station, and if you didn't fill the wagons that day, your contract was void.

At the same time, you could only pull the beet and top it a few days before the wagons arrived, or the beet would dry up and lose sugar content.

Around the time of the harvest in October 1964, we had the foulest weather you can imagine. We were hit by howling wind, torrential rain and plunging temperatures with frost and snow. We didn't manage to pull all the beet.

I recall trying to sneak past my parents' bedroom after arriving back from a dance at 2.30am that same morning the wagons were due to arrive.

My dad called me.

"What's it like outside tonight, Sean?" he asked.

"It's very cold, but it's dry," I said.

"Get changed," he said. *"We'll go pull the rest of the beet."*

We pulled all night, and when it got light, we topped it with large knives. The tractor and trailers came at 9.00am, and we loaded beet all day.

There was no need for a gym in those days.

He had a favourite saying when he'd see me flagging a bit.

"Don't ever let it be said your mother reared a jibber (quitter)," he'd say.

It still comes to mind whenever I feel like giving up on something.

My mother Mary was from a farming background and was a great support to my father working in the fields too. I worked alongside her in the fields most evenings after school and during holidays as often as I did with my father.

My dad did his best to imbue me with his moral values and try to lead me along the spiritual path he followed.

I often remember him telling me how we should *"always have a great care for the orphan and the widow."*

When my best friend, Mick Corcoran's dad died, my father took care of him and his widowed mother as if they were his own family.

There was no fanfare about it. He wouldn't think of behaving any other way because he was a charitable and kind man to his marrow.

I spent summers working with him, cutting earthen-brown blocks of turf from the bog and saving the hay on sunshine August days.

It was back-breaking work, but I loved working with my father. He was such a positive influence and seemed to revel in the simplicity of being alive.

Liz was so like him. She touched and enriched the lives of everyone she met. She radiated a great sense of peace and happiness and warmth. She had a smile that could melt the coldest soul.

Yet for a long time, I resisted joining her in that rich and happy world. I stayed out of reach of her warm and caring embrace and lived in my own dark and frozen fury.

3

Virgin Mary Locution

"Behold, I stand at the door [of your heart] and knock.
He who hears my voice and opens the door, I will come into him."
Revelation 3:20

While I was busy being Mr. Angry, Liz worked hard to provide us with a peaceful atmosphere at home.

She made the house into our own little haven from the world.

Meanwhile, I drank more than I should have, and I know I was an embarrassment to her at times.

Among the many things Liz did was arrange all our holidays. After the children died, the only holidays we wanted to take were pilgrimages.

We wanted to be anywhere that brought us closer to heaven, to where God and our children were.

Instead of destinations like China, America and Russia, we wanted to be in spiritual places like Lourdes, Fatima, the Holy Land.

But if I was hard to live with, I was even harder to travel with. When it rained, I would blow up; if the flight was delayed, I would explode; if the hotel room wasn't perfect, I'd create a scene.

My anger was seldom directed at Liz, but she felt it intensely all the same. She was gentle and reserved by nature, so I embarrassed her when I shouted and behaved like an idiot in public.

She never lectured me, but she let me know that I was not being the type of person our children would be proud of.

Yet, I continued on like this for years. I would feel ashamed at times, but then I'd do the exact same thing again.

Then one day I looked at Liz, and I could see she was stressed, and I was to blame. It dawned on me that she was walking on egg shells because of me.

She was trying to cope with my emotional baggage and working hard to make a peaceful life for us. Meanwhile, I was acting like a child having a permanent temper tantrum.

I wasn't happy, and as a result, I was making Liz, the person I loved most in the world, unhappy as well.

It was like my own little Road to Damascus moment. I didn't want to be the angry, immature person that I was anymore.

I made up my mind that I'd be inspired by my calm and peaceful wife.

I remembered my father too, and how he was similar in temperament to Liz. He was and is my hero, and I wanted to be more like him.

That day, I promised Liz that I was on the road to being a better person. I warned her that I was a work in progress, but I vowed to her that I was going to change.

She deserved a better, more caring man in her life, and I wanted that man to be me.

Once I made that commitment to be more like Liz and my father, I embarked on a new direction in life.

I paused; I counted to ten, and I thought before I reacted. It was only then that I began what became a spiritual journey.

I'm a slow learner, but with Liz as my guide and inspiration, I persisted in trying to change.

My behaviour and my feelings began to evolve, and I felt better and happier.

I continued reading and reasoning about religion, philosophy and science. I educated myself about world belief systems and the fundamentals of all the religions.

Once the anger began fading, I started to think more and see more clearly.

I think those whisperings in my soul grew louder and when I really thought about it, I realised that in my heart I always knew there was a Divine Creator.

If I believed in a Divine Creator who made everything in this world, I had to believe there was a purpose behind it; that he had something in mind for us.

And if he went to all this trouble and there was a purpose behind it, he would probably leave a handbook or a guide to tell us what it's all about.

The only book which comes anywhere close to that is the Bible.

So I was drawn to Christianity again, and within Christianity, it was the values and teachings of the Catholic faith that still resonated with me.

The Catholic faith's interpretation of the New Testament is the closest we get on earth to the truth and the teachings of Jesus.

I was still a long way from being like Liz or my father, but I stopped acting like the tantrum-throwing child. I was maturing at last and starting to feel a greater sense of inner peace.

But I was still far from perfect. I had 'L' plates on when it came to the spiritual world, and I could easily be diverted down a wrong road.

In my forties, I landed a high-octane job as director of manufacturing with the blue-chip U.S. firm, Hewlett Packard. I was responsible for the technology transfer to Ireland and for the start-up of the operations here in 1995.

Based in Dublin, the job also involved a lot of business travel around Europe, America and Asia.

I didn't enjoy travelling much without Liz. We saved my air miles so she would travel with me at times, and we would take a holiday at the end of the business trip.

By 2003, I was 56-years-old, and I was preparing to put my feet up by taking early retirement. We were financially secure and the time was right.

Liz and I had lots of plans to go travelling, play more golf and see more of the world.

The company's move to Ireland was such a success that management offered a generous golden handshake for my contributions.

They said I could avail of the package anytime over the coming years.

Our retirement looked rosy. We planned to sell our house in Dublin and move back to the country and live happily ever after.

Then I got news that rocked me to the core. I discovered that tax advice I'd received years earlier from the best financial accountants was flawed.

It looked like we owed a lot of money to the Revenue Commissioners. The tax man was going to take our investments and wipe out all our savings.

This devastated me. It jeopardised everything I had worked for and dreamed of. I knew we wouldn't end up living under a bridge, but the luxurious lifestyle I envisaged for our retirement crumbled before my eyes.

All my newfound peace and serenity disappeared overnight with the news. I was in a bad way; I couldn't see straight. This was a real blow to my confidence and my sense of security.

Liz tried to make me see sense and insisted we had more than enough to live on without the savings.

"Once we have one another, we can deal with whatever life throws at us," she said, yet again.

But I had no sense of perspective about it at all. I couldn't think about anything else, and I became obsessed with the money that I was about to lose.

This was a crisis, a total disaster for me. I even called out in desperation to Our Lady to help me.

Liz tried to get me to relax, but I even lost interest in golf. I couldn't concentrate on the game, and I tried to explain to her that I couldn't face even having an ordinary conversation with people.

"We'll go somewhere else to play golf, and then you won't have to talk to anyone we know," Liz decided. *"You need to calm down, Sean. This is not good for you."*

So Liz drove us to a public golf course called Pine Trees in Clane, County Kildare one Sunday afternoon. I didn't want to go, but Liz wasn't taking no for an answer.

The looming tax bill was all I could see in my mind's eye. I fretted and belly-ached to myself in between hitting the golf ball and praying to Our Lady to help me.

At one hole on this course, the ladies' and gents' tees were a good distance from the other, and a copse of trees separated Liz and me.

She was out of sight and earshot, and there wasn't another soul around me on the course. I was completely alone.

That tax bill was still running through my head, and I muttered distracted prayers to Our Lady at the same time. There wasn't a breath of air, and all was quiet around me.

Out of nowhere, I experienced what's called 'a locution' or an internal message.

I heard a voice which I believed to be the Blessed Virgin saying, *"Peace, be at peace, be at peace."*

I heard the voice in my head as plain as if someone was standing beside me whispering the words in my ear. I read a lot about other people having locution experiences, but nothing like this had happened to me before.

I wondered if I'd imagined it, but my first reaction was frustration. I thought: *"What kind of rubbish advice is this?"*

"How can I be at peace?" I argued. *"How can I find peace of mind in this world? After losing our children, I struggled for years to be at peace with your Son's will.*

"I've just achieved a sense of peace in my life with Liz's support.

"Now as we're about to retire, it looks like all our savings will be wiped out. How am I supposed to be at peace?"

Then I heard the calm response:

"Your peace in this world will be your developing relationship with my Son, through me and the little things you can do for Liz."

I found myself repeating the words over and over again. I wasn't quite sure what Our Lady meant, but I felt a sudden sense of peace again.

Relief flooded through me. I suddenly realised: *"'What am I worried about? This money is not important. God is in my life, and He loves me. I have Liz. I have so much to be grateful for already."*

Liz saw a new man when she caught up with me on the golf course. I was smiling, laughing, breathless and maybe a bit wild-eyed telling her about the locution.

Liz had great faith, but she wasn't a person for believing in moving statues, speaking in tongues or indeed, speaking with the Virgin Mary.

She listened and nodded and probably thought: *"I hope he's not losing it, but I'm glad if it gives him a little peace of mind."*

The strange thing is that the tax situation resolved itself within the next few months. I did owe some tax but nothing as high as I'd feared earlier.

Then money came in from other investments that rose in value during the boom. It was a windfall that I wasn't expecting at all and made up for the tax losses.

The impending disaster never happened.

In thanksgiving, we decided to visit the Marian Shrine in Knock in Mayo for a weekend. We went to Knock once or twice a year, but this occasion was in special thanks for my locution from the Virgin Mary.

As we reached the shrine gate, a man stepped before me to offer a leaflet on the Divine Mercy Devotion. I had heard of it, but I knew very little about it.

Our Lady's words about the *"developing relationship with my Son, through me"* was at the forefront of my mind. I interpreted the leaflet as a message from the Virgin telling me how to get closer to her Son.

After that, I learnt all I could about Divine Mercy Devotion.

The devotion began when Polish nun, Sister Faustina, had an apparition of Our Lord in the 1930s.

He promised that he would give Divine Mercy to any sinner that repents their sins, no matter how grave.

Jesus told St. Faustina that *"every soul believing and trusting in His mercy will obtain it."*

He asked that a feast day be dedicated to his Divine Mercy and celebrated on the Sunday after Easter.

The former Pope John Paul II, now Saint John Paul II, canonised Sister Faustina in April 2000.

Since then, the second Sunday of Easter is known throughout the Church as Divine Mercy Sunday.

The Chaplet of Divine Mercy is a powerful prayer recited using ordinary rosary beads. It has two opening prayers from the Diary of Saint Faustina, followed by a closing prayer.

It's encouraged to recite the Chaplet at 3.00pm, the Hour of Great Mercy and the time of Christ's death on the cross.

So, I started saying the Divine Mercy Chaplet every day at the appointed hour. I got great peace from this and felt that I was following Our Lady's instructions, and getting closer to her Son through her.

My devotion to the prayer eventually led us to Poland where we visited the Divine Mercy sites for my 60th birthday.

Meanwhile, I did continue to wonder what the Virgin Mary had meant about *"the little things"* I could do for Liz.

I thought it was Our Lady's way of saying that Liz didn't need all the money or grand things that I thought I was providing for her.

I knew that Our Lady was right. Liz would have lived in a tent with me if I lost all our money. She never cared about possessions, only people.

I retired in 2006, and we sold our house in Lucan in Dublin which had increased significantly in value during the property boom.

We traded down to a comfortable, smaller house in Rathvilly, in Carlow. It was close to Liz's widowed mother, and we loved the area.

We travelled, played golf together and did all the things we had planned to do during my retirement.

After our early years of grief and trauma, it seemed that we were set to live a charmed life in our sunset years.

Liz and I were happier and closer than ever.

Then just over one year after I retired, in April 2008, doctors shattered us with news that Liz had cancer.

Dark clouds gathered on the horizon, and we knew that our lives were about to change forever.

Reflection on the Locution from the Virgin Mary

Looking back now, the prospect of losing our life savings was a grace from God, albeit a very distressing one for me at the time.

It was a grace granted to me to teach me the error of worshipping material things.

My huge sense of distress wasn't even rational as our life savings weren't everything we owned.

We were very well off compared to many people. We had a very valuable house in Dublin which we were planning to sell on my retirement. We planned to buy a much smaller house down the country less than half the price.

I had an excellent private pension, and I was due a good severance package from Hewlett Packard.

We had enough money for a comfortable retirement without our savings. Liz knew this and tried hard to help me see this.

But my over-reaction to this threat was all about greed and an obsession with material things.

The prospect of losing our savings melted away soon after this experience on the golf course.

I cleaned up the mess I'd made of my tax affairs, and everything was resolved with no negative impact.

All the panic seemed so foolish. Even if I had to pay out all that money, it wouldn't have mattered because we didn't need it.

But as it says in the book of Ecclesiastes 5:10 *"Whoever loves money never has enough; whoever loves wealth is never satisfied with their income."*

I wanted it, but I didn't need it.

I realised afterwards that I had lost all sense of perspective and forgot to value what was important.

This was never more evident than in the months after Liz's cancer diagnosis. The whole experience taught me about the pointlessness of material idolatry.

It also reminded me how easy it is to make the wrong decisions in a time of financial stress.

I opened myself to a significant tax exposure through imprudence and greed, and I could have chosen to go down an even worse route.

I could have tried to lie and hide the problem from Revenue, but that wasn't even an option once I told Liz. She didn't care what it cost, as long as we did the right thing.

But it has been my experience in 40 years of business that many people take the wrong path when they reach this fork in the road.

We know from the financial crash that people make mistakes. But they make things worse when they make the wrong decisions and try to conceal their errors.

They can throw good money after bad or throw more fuel on the fire, and then everything spirals out of control.

It all came back to me when I was writing a homily on the Parable of the Unjust Steward from Luke 16:1-13.

Jesus tells a story about a boss (the master) and his manager (the steward) who are both unsavoury characters.

The rich master tells his business manager that he's firing him. The manager isn't conscientious about looking after his boss's affairs and has wasted money.

Realising that he will soon be out of work, the manager starts to curry favour with other businessmen who owe money to his boss.

With a stroke of his pen, he reduces what they owe to his master in exchange for work and shelter when he loses his job.

So, from being incompetent in his job, he makes matters worse by being dishonest too. Yet when the master learns what 'the unjust steward' has done, he commends him for his "shrewdness."

Jesus explains the parable by saying: *"For the sons of this world are more shrewd in dealing with their own generation than the sons of light"* (Luke 16:8).

By "sons of this world", Jesus means unbelievers while the "sons of light" are the believers.

The unjust steward cheats his master so he will get access to other homes. The master, who is also an unbeliever, is so obsessed with money that he even admires the fraudster who cheated him.

Jesus wants His followers to be Just Stewards rather than Unjust ones. The Unjust Steward sees his master's resources as a means for his own personal gain.

Jesus wants His followers to use the resources that our Master gives us for the benefit of others than ourselves.

He encourages His followers to share their wealth in this life so that in the next life they will be received *"into eternal dwellings."*

He is asking us to take care of the poor and the vulnerable, who in return will welcome us through the gates of heaven.

Jesus finishes the lesson in verse 13: *"No servant can serve two masters, for either he will hate the one and love the other, or he will be devoted to the one and despise the other. You cannot serve God and money."*

The Gospel according to Matthew 6:21, says Jesus continues the discussion of wealth during the Sermon on the Mount.

Jesus explains that believers should store their treasure in heaven rather than on earth.

He warns that if our treasure is on earth, our focus and attention will also be on earthly matters, to the exclusion of God.

In other words, focusing on money in this life is futile when compared to eternity.

We should focus on real treasures which are our values in life, the welfare of others and our spiritual welfare.

Jesus explains: *"For where your treasure is, there your heart will be also."*

If we focus on real values, we are not likely to be drawn on the wrong path.

We are also less likely to be wasteful - not just financially - but with our God-given talents and gifts including our actions, our time and our words.

Saint Paul, in a letter to the Galatians 6:7, states this more elegantly than I ever can:

"A man will reap what he sows; if nature is his seed ground, nature will give him a perishable harvest; if his seed-ground is the spirit, it will give him a harvest of eternal life."

I was greedy and distracted by too many worldly things and by His grace, I found my real values and treasures.

We all need to be Just Stewards looking after all our Master has given us in His name.

We are all supposed to use the gifts, talents and resources that are God-given to help those less fortunate.

Let us pray that He will give all of us the grace to be his children of light rather than children of this world.

Happy times on a night out together

4

Liz's Illness

*"Even though I walk through the darkest valley, I will fear no evil,
for you are with me; your rod and your staff, they comfort me."*
Psalms 23:4

It all started so innocently. There was nothing sinister about Liz's illness at all in the beginning. She said she felt a little niggle in her side; that was it.

She wondered if she'd strained something while doing the gardening or while golfing. I thought it was gallstones, and that she might need shockwave treatment to break them up.

She went to the doctor when the ache didn't go away, and he referred her for an MRI scan at a clinic in Kilkenny.

We thought we'd kill two birds with one stone, and I got my eyes tested there the same day. I had my eyes checked at the optician's, and there was concern that I might be losing a bit of my field of vision.

In fact, Liz was far more concerned about my eyes that her own ailment when we went to the clinic that morning.

She wasn't bothered about that faint pain in her side. Neither of us worried about there being anything serious.

I was down the hall from Liz in another consulting room in the clinic, and we emerged around the same time. I had a spring in my step. They told me there was nothing wrong with my eyesight at all.

I was delighted until I saw her face, and I knew straight away that something was wrong.

"What did they say, Liz? What's wrong?"

Liz shrugged it off.

"Let's go down to the cafeteria and get lunch, and I'll tell you then. What about your eyes?"

When we sat down, she told me that the radiographer who read her scan couldn't hide his shock. Usually, they only write a report to the doctor detailing their findings.

He said that three-quarters of her kidney was destroyed. He apologised for his reaction but urged her not to delay returning to her doctor. He said he would send the full report straight away.

He never mentioned the word cancer to her, but she knew.

She got referred to a nephrologist or kidney consultant who confirmed it was cancer. In no time, Liz was in Tallaght Hospital having the remains of the kidney removed.

The consultant explained that to ensure they got all the cancer, they dug in and pulled up, turned around and checked through everything.

"Your system is going to be upset for a while," he warned.

Liz was continually getting sick, but they'd already told us to expect this.

When the worst of the sickness eased off, Liz was discharged.

The doctors put her on a new oral drug rather than chemo. We went home to Rathvilly full of hope for the future.

From the start, we agreed that we'd go to all the appointments together and discuss everything with the doctors only when both of us was present.

The idea was that there would never be anything that Liz knew that I didn't or vice versa.

We were a team, and we were tackling this head on together. Whatever they told us, we would deal with it.

We were back and forward to the hospital for scans and appointments

Around June or July, we went back to see the consultant. The news seemed positive. Things were going as well as could be expected, they told us.

I've learnt since that they only tell you as much as you want to know. The medics like to leave you with hope, so we left the hospital still feeling naively optimistic.

We visited Our Lady's shrine in Knock in late summer. We always found it a special and prayerful experience, so we visited a couple of times every year.

Knock Shrine has a well-stocked religious bookstore where I liked to browse. I'd always pick up a book or two whenever we visited.

Sometimes, Liz and I read a monthly magazine published by an Irish priest called the Curate's Diary. It often printed 'messages from heaven' from a woman who calls herself Anne, a Lay Apostle.

She says she receives locutions from God, and she has published books on her messages from Jesus. I didn't know much about her apart that she lives in Ireland and she gets some support from her local bishop.

I'd noted down the name of one of her books, and I came across it in the bookshop in Knock.

It's a book called the Mist of Mercy, and I decided to buy it along with a couple of other books including one on Saint Teresa of Calcutta.

A few months later, Liz started to feel more unwell. The pain and the sickness that the doctors attributed to the operation did not go away.

Her breathing was terrible too, but they had warned us to expect that.

Around November, she ended up back in the hospital for a few weeks and even needed an oxygen tank for a while.

"It's just a setback; Liz needs to be stabilised," I thought.

Then one day, I was with Liz when her consultant and his team arrived on their ward rounds. They had Liz's latest charts and test results, and the consultant was blunt.

"I'm afraid, we've got bad news. The drug isn't working. It works for some people, but in your case, it's not doing its job."

We were dazed by this news. The way he said it, it sounded like there was no real alternative to the treatment.

It was the first sign that we had that this might be terminal.

I could see how upset and shocked Liz was. In the end, I asked the consultant and his team to leave, I wanted some time alone with her.

After the doctors went away, she turned to me and said: *"Why me, Sean? Why is it always me?"*

I hugged her and said: *"I don't know Liz, I really don't know."*

It is the only time in our 40 years together that I ever heard her question or complain. It's the only time she showed she was human after all.

Within half an hour, she was back to her stoic old self, and she never complained or never questioned anything again.

Through Liz's example and support over the years, my faith and spirituality had developed and deepened. I prayed for the strength to allow me to support Liz in the way she deserved through this time.

But I felt desperately scared. I didn't know if I could do what she needed. I wanted to do something, anything for her but I felt helpless.

A day or two later, I bumped into her consultant again on the corridor, and I asked him: *"Is that it? Is there nothing you can do?"*

"Yes, of course, we have options," he said then. *"We can try chemotherapy. I have to warn you that I wouldn't be hugely optimistic but it does work in some cases."*

I went back to Liz's bed feeling jubilant. We both saw chemo as an unexpected light in what had been a dark tunnel.

Liz went to mass and devotions and was a great believer, but she never read much on religion. She'd read books on flowers, gardening and cookery but never picked up any of my religious books around the house.

I read the Bible, but to be honest, I preferred to read about the lives of the saints.

Their belief in God and how they lived their lives fascinated me.

Liz wouldn't read the biographies, but I'd tell her about each book I was reading, and she always enjoyed the stories too.

We were both feeling low because we knew when she left the hospital, she was facing chemo. The chemo offered a sliver of hope.

But even then, we knew in our hearts that there was little chance of it working.

Our conversations, which usually flowed, reduced to a trickle, and Liz found it difficult to read in the hospital.

I took out the Mist of Mercy, the book that I'd bought in Knock and started to read parts of it to her.

As we tried to come to terms with the inevitable, the book turned out to be an interesting diversion.

The book is about Anne the Lay Apostle's visions and insights into hell, heaven and purgatory.

Liz and I had never discussed the constructs of the afterlife. In our heads and hearts, Seana and Kieran and our parents were in heaven, and we both hoped to go where they are.

But we'd never discussed the actual construct, the physical and metaphysical reality of the afterlife. You don't generally, do you?

In her book, Anne the Lay Apostle claims Jesus has provided her with an insight into life after death.

Part of the book deals with heaven and what a beautiful place it is. You wouldn't mind dying for it right now.

She gives a horrific description of hell which is filled with damned souls suffering for eternity.

But most of the book is about purgatory where most people are destined for unless they're saints or very evil.

Anne the Lay Apostle explains that everyone is in purgatory to work out all the issues that made them sinners on earth.

There are also many different levels of purgatory. She says if you've sinned a lot, you'll end up beside the gates of hell, where it'll take forever to get up towards the light and the gates of heaven.

She explains that when someone prays for you on earth, you can get move faster through purgatory.

Or you could end up somewhere in the middle of purgatory because you weren't too bad at all on earth.

The person who goes to purgatory and lands a place near the gates of heaven has it best of all. They can't leave until they've done their time, but all their loved ones can come from heaven and visit them.

As I read the book aloud, it was clear in my mind where Liz would be after she died. I knew my fate was nowhere as certain.

"Well, you don't need to worry anyway, you'll be directed straight to heaven on arrival," I said. *"Please, don't forget about me."*

Liz shook her head and insisted she had plenty of faults and imperfections like all of us.

"I hope I've never done anything bad enough to merit being behind the gates of hell," she mused. *"But if it's like Anne the Lay Apostle says, I could end up at the halfway mark in purgatory."*

"And once I can get above halfway, I'll be closer to where Seana and Kieran are."

We spent hours reading the book and discussing its claims and insights. It was a source of fascination for us.

After being discharged, Liz started on a regime of chemo.

She'd go in once a week to Tallaght Hospital for the treatment, and it was tough on her. Her hair started going light, and she had all the usual side effects of nausea and terrible fatigue.

I tried to ignore the obvious signs and talked about things that we'd do together when she recovered. But we both felt she wasn't getting any better with the chemo.

Around this time, I woke up in bed with a start in the middle of the night. I was half asleep, half-awake but I felt something had disturbed me.

It was then I saw the shadow pass in the bedroom.

It was more of a sense than anything that it was Liz's sister Mary. I saw an outline of her in her habit like the photo on her memorial cards.

She went to Liz's side and looked down at her sleeping baby sister. Then she went to move away again, but as she left, I heard her message: *"Liz has a journey to go on, and you can help, but you can't be on it."*

She knew I didn't want to let Liz go, and she knew that Liz was worried about leaving me behind. I was always the pessimist. I didn't think I was able for this.

My one prayer was: *"Lord, give me the strength."*

So, it was like Mary warning me: *"If you don't have the strength, you better find it. You can help her, but if you can't, don't get in her way."*

I didn't tell Liz at the time because I was afraid that it might frighten her. It frightened me. People have asked if I dreamt it, and maybe I did, but it was very distinct for me.

Then on Saturday, December 13, Liz became very ill with nausea and retching. The hospital had told us to go to A&E if anything like that happened.

When we got to Tallaght Hospital, they admitted her quickly.

She was so sick that for the first time I understood that the cancer had spread. I suspected that it had reached her stomach, and her breathing was so bad, it must have been in her lungs.

Her doctors worked hard to stabilise her condition again, and when Liz seemed a bit better, I left the ward for a few minutes.

I only got outside the door, when the locum beckoned at me to come to the nurses' station.

I knew it wasn't good news by his grave expression, but I didn't believe Liz's medical condition could get much worse.

Then the doctor began to up update me on her condition, and I realised I was wrong.

He said that Liz's surviving kidney had stopped working from the violence of the nausea and dehydration.

After everything she'd been through with cancer, I couldn't believe this was happening to her now.

He said that they were going to try and get the kidney restarted over the weekend with a combination of intravenous fluids and drugs.

It was the first time that I'd heard distressing news like this without Liz being present.

It meant I had to do the last thing in the world I wanted to do - I had to go back in and tell Liz.

The hospital moved her into a private room straight away. I was ashen-faced and trembling; Liz was calm and accepting.

They put her on a drip, and all weekend I watched the bag that they connected to her. I prayed for liquid gold to appear in it because it would be a sign that the kidney had restarted.

Because of the tragedies early in our marriage, we were exceptionally close as a couple. When anything serious happened to us, we circled the wagons, held each other tightly and faced it together.

Liz never liked sharing her troubles with others, so we dealt with this news by ourselves.

Once she moved into the private room, I started staying in the hospital around the clock. They gave me a camp bed so I could sleep beside her.

At least I wasn't at a loss on how to talk to Liz anymore.

What conversations do you have when death looks imminent?

There is nothing about this material world that's worth talking about, especially if your children and parents are already in heaven.

Nothing mattered anymore - not money, not sports, not the house, not holidays, not religion, not politics, not the weather. There was nothing in this world of interest to us.

We just picked up where we left off talking about the Mists of Mercy.

It was a wonderful consolation to be able to talk, laugh and speculate about what happens to us in the afterlife. We both knew that's where Liz was going soon.

Even if her surviving kidney started to work again, it was just a matter of time before cancer took her.

I wanted the prospect of death to be as comforting as it could be for Liz, and she wanted the same for me.

She knew I was hoping to follow her very soon, so we both wanted to consider what would happen to us.

I felt that I wouldn't be far behind, once Liz went. I hoped that a stroke or a heart attack would take me as fast as possible.

I wasn't worried about it, and I wasn't being morbid. I didn't care how I died as long as it would get me on my way. I wanted to be on the next bus.

I would never do anything stupid, but that's my feelings to this day - I'd be happy to go in the morning.

Together Liz and I worked out wonderful constructs about what might happen after we died. We were engrossed in it.

We talked about seeing Seana and Kieran again. How incredible it would be if they could come out and meet us.

"I wouldn't mind how long I stayed in purgatory then," said Liz. *"I could stay as long as it took, once I could see them sometimes."*

We talked about how wonderful it would be for her to see her father,

Tom and mother, Margaret, again. She could see her older sister, Mary and her older brother, Jim, too after all those years.

We started thinking about those visits from her family, and soon we couldn't stop laughing.

Liz's father and older sister were quiet and conservative people, and her mother and older brother were the opposite. Margaret and Jim were larger than life with big hearty laughs.

When they went into a room full of silent strangers, they'd leave with a gang of noisy friends.

We couldn't imagine how these two party people were coping if heaven is a tranquil and peaceful place.

We thought how Liz's dad and sister must be all the time warning her mother and brother to keep down the noise.

We created all these daft scenarios and mad conversations for Liz's family and mine when they came to visit us in purgatory.

We spent the weekend laughing and dreaming and creating these family mini-dramas in our heads.

From being almost at a total loss at the time Liz needed me the most, I couldn't have been closer to her.

I believe that the book, Mist of Mercy, was given to me to console her.

It meant I could do what she had done for me during all through our years of married life: I was able to support her and comfort her during her worst days.

I thank Jesus for this grace every day, and will until the day I die and forever after.

On the Monday, the doctors came in, and there was liquid in the bag.

I joked with Liz and the doctor: *"I'm never so glad to see a bag of piss in all my life!"*

Our euphoria was short-lived because they came back and told us that the liquid wasn't from the kidney. It hadn't restarted at all.

The nightmare scenario became a reality as they told us that neither dialysis nor a transplant was an option for Liz.

When the kidneys are gone, we were told that death inevitably follows within a few days.

So that was it; we were on a countdown. In the space of minutes, this world had become a very bleak place indeed.

5

Last Days with Liz

"There is a time for everything,
and a season for every activity under the heavens:
a time to be born and a time to die,
a time to plant and a time to uproot,
a time to kill and a time to heal,
a time to tear down and a time to build,
a time to weep and a time to laugh,
a time to mourn and a time to dance…"
Ecclesiastes 3:1-6

Liz was always organised and calm, and even though she had been issued a death sentence, she was unflappable. She was never one for chaos or melodrama, and she wasn't going to start now.

The doctors had estimated that Liz had three days to live, plus or minus a few hours.

They also assured us it would be relatively painless. The toxins would gradually overwhelm her system, and it would be a slow and gentle drift into unconsciousness.

Father John Kelly was the Catholic chaplain to the hospital. His main job was the pastoral care of the neighbouring parish, so he wasn't in the hospital all the time.

He came in that day to hear Liz's confession and to give her holy communion. We chatted with him, and we told him Liz was likely to be in heaven by Thursday.

We knew we had to start breaking the news to our families and a few close friends, but even this was carefully organised by Liz.

She didn't want everyone pouring in at once, and she wanted me to set up a rota so that she'd have time to say goodbye to everyone.

Meanwhile, I told Liz about some experiences I had that I hadn't shared with her before this.

A few days earlier, I had experienced a wonderful vision of Seana coming out of heaven to meet her mother.

To explain the vision properly, I have to divert a bit and describe one of Liz's mannerisms.

Every week without fail, we visited the cemetery, and part of this weekly routine involved Liz preparing flowers in the back kitchen.

It was a tight space, and she had vases, water and flowers everywhere.

Of course, precisely at that time, I'd need something in there. And I was like the bull in a China shop, sending things crashing without meaning to.

So, as soon as I tried to get into the back kitchen, I'd get Liz's two erect palms facing me.

This was like a flashing red light. There was no conversation, and there were no words needed.

Those two palms meant: *"Do not come any further. Retreat now."*

Much as she loved me, flowers for her loved ones in the cemetery were precious too, and when something was important to Liz, I knew all about it.

The palms of her hands meant a categorical, clear-cut *'no'*.

Our daughter Seana was gentle and funny like her mother, but she also had that same steely determination when something was important to her.

You were never in any doubt when something was important to Seana.

So, in this vision, I saw Seana waiting to meet Liz. She had Kieran by the hand. Liz's mother and father and her sister and brother were advancing behind the children.

And then I saw Seana turn around to them with her palms raised.

It was clear to me then that Seana was telling them all: *"No! I'm going to take Mammy's hand first. No one else is doing it."*

This was important to Seana, and she was letting everyone know. She had waited 33 years for this moment, and no one was going to take it from her.

I kept the vision to myself for days because I hoped it was premature and that Seana wouldn't be taking Liz's hand for a long time.

But now that death was imminent, I told Liz about the two visions I'd kept from her.

I told her first about the story of her sister's visit to her that night many weeks earlier.

Then I told her about my vision of Seana and Kieran.

They were huge, huge consolations for her. She hoped that was how it was going to be. She could picture it now.

Friends and family started arriving as scheduled.

I tried to leave enough time between each visit for Liz to rest so she could rally in time for the next one. She wanted to be alert as she could to see everyone for the last time.

No one's final visit was rushed, but it was final. Liz didn't want anyone coming back because she felt it would be too difficult to have to say goodbye over and over again.

The next time they came to see Liz, it would be her funeral

She was clear that she wanted her last day to be for the two of us on our own.

Liz also didn't want the visits to be weepy and maudlin. So, we told everyone about the Mist of Mercy and the conversations we'd been having about reuniting with all who had passed.

We related our stories about Liz's family coming to meet her when she passed over and the ructions that she'd face in the greeting party.

We talked about my vision of Seana meeting Liz which made everyone smile.

That's how it was. There was nothing morbid or grim about it. I would let Liz tell as much of each story as she was able, and if she got tired, I'd finish it for her.

Everyone laughed and cried and said their goodbyes but left knowing Liz was at peace.

They could see she was happy at the prospect of seeing Seana, Kieran and her family again. Liz's only concern was for me.

From early on, Liz became less mobile and increasingly bedbound as the toxins flooded her system.

All the nursing staff at Tallaght Hospital were caring, but from the start, we had two night nurses who were our special angels of mercy.

Bright, cheerful and chatty, they were so attentive to Liz, and they seemed as if they had all the time in the world to look after her.

We had photos of our two children on the wall, and they wanted to know all about them. Of course, we couldn't stop talking about Seana and Kieran.

Those girls brought colour from the outside world into the sterile hospital room every time they arrived.

Liz needed the pillows fluffed up and rearranged around her every few hours, as her joints got stiffer and more uncomfortable.

I tried boxing those pillows into place, but I could have done it for a week, and I still wouldn't have got it right.

Those nurses came in, applied their magic touch and in seconds made Liz comfortable again.

They discussed finding one of those electronic, adjustable beds which would enable Liz to change position with the flick of a remote control.

They promised that hell or high water they would find one of those beds for Liz.

The next morning the bed arrived. It meant for Liz's remaining days I could use the remote control anytime during the day or night to help her find relief.

The third morning came, and we knew this was likely to be Liz's last day on earth. She was weaker but still alert.

But she was also sore and tender all over, and she dreaded having the daily bed bath when the new shift came on.

She never said anything, but I could see she found it very painful, and I'd ask the nurses to be careful.

That morning, however, our two favourite night nurses came in at the time they usually finished their shift.

"Liz, we're going to give you the bed bath today," one of them announced cheerily.

They must have decided to stay on at the end of their night shift to do this.

Usually, the other nurses suggested I go away while they got on with the job. But these girls urged me to stay as they chatted away with Liz.

They were so gentle and unhurried that she hardly knew it was happening.

When they finished, one of them picked up Liz's bottle of perfume on the side table. It was her signature perfume which hadn't been touched since we arrived in hospital.

Called *'Knowing'* by Estee Lauder, it's a kind of warm, woody fragrance. As the girls sprayed her, they marvelled at the scent.

"Oh, Liz, that's a beautiful perfume. I never came across a scent like that," said one of them.

I told them that I was always under instruction to pick it up when I was passing in the duty-free.

"You've done well for yourself, Liz. You've still got him buying you lovely perfume after all these years. Where did you meet Sean?"

"We'd love to meet a man like that. We're always finding useless boyfriends…"

We told them about The Dreamland where we met, and we had all this kind of light-hearted banter between us.

"I'm telling you, Liz, they don't make them like Sean anymore. A friend of mine has a boyfriend who arrived up with a few chocolates for her the other night, and then he sat down and ate the lot of them himself..,"

We talked about the children again, and we told them about Seana coming to take Liz's hand when she passed over.

It was a lovely chat mostly between the nurses and Liz. I was a supporting cast member only.

So finally, the girls were leaving, and Liz and I knew we were unlikely to see them again.

I'm dreadful with names. If I mix up a name at the beginning, I'm done for because I can never get it right in my head after that.

Their names were Niamh and Lorna, and somehow, I'd got it in my head that they were Niamh and Orla.

As they were going out the door, I said goodbye to them and added: *"Thanks so much Niamh; thanks for everything, Orla!"*

Liz looked confused and asked: *"Sean, is she called Orla or Lorna?"*

The girls stopped at the door, and the one I addressed as Orla replied: *"Don't mind him, Liz. You're right, my name's Lorna."*

Liz had a tremendous regard for them. She was only hours from death, yet she wanted me to get their names right.

I didn't know then, but a few years later I was so thankful that she did.

Somebody came in to take bloods after the nurses left, but we sent them packing.

"Vampires!" I said. *"Get out!"*

Father John came back to anoint Liz with the last rites. We were able to tell him we were reconciled to God's will. The truth was, of course, that Liz was far more reconciled than I was.

We told him all about Seana and Kieran and how their mother looked forward to their imminent reunion.

No one disturbed us after that.

The doctors disappeared, and Liz seemed drowsy, so I thought it would be a good time to put on some soothing music.

I had brought some of Liz's favourite hymns of Our Lady and a CD player.

"Liz," I said. *"I'm going to put on Our Lady of Knock for you."*

The gentle tune with its lyrics of *"Golden Rose, Queen of Ireland, all my cares and troubles cease"* played softly in the room.

Liz muttered something that I couldn't make out, so I repeated it.

"Liz, love, I'm just playing Our Lady of Knock for you."

Again, Liz muttered something which I could not make out. Her voice was very indistinct now.

I prayed: *"Oh Lord, let me understand what Liz is saying."*

I didn't want to keep bothering her, but I didn't want to miss what might be her final words.

So, for a third time, I whispered to Liz, that her favourite hymn was playing.

Then Liz sat bolt upright in the bed and fixed me with those still striking blue eyes.

"That's nice, Sean," she said. *"But make sure you don't have them on too loud. There are very sick people on this floor!"*

She knew that I wasn't the most sensitive person when it came to the needs of people around me.

She was afraid that I'd have the music blaring and disturb people around us. I didn't, but it wasn't past me to do something stupid like that.

Even when she was dying, Liz was still concerned about everyone else.

We prayed, talked and listened to the hymns all morning. I recited the Divine Mercy and the Rosary with Liz, and then we'd chat some more.

But I could see, as the hours ticked by, that I had to do more and more of the talking. Liz was tired and drowsy, but at the same time, I could see she was listening.

I took the photographs of the children off the wall. One was of Seana on her tricycle, and the other was Kieran as a tiny baby.

I placed them on her chest and took her hands to show her where they were.

My brother P.J. arrived in for a few minutes in the afternoon. He wanted to make sure I got something to eat.

He and Liz were alike in a lot of ways, and they were very close. He said a few quiet words to Liz, and then said he was going down to the chapel for a while.

He knew 3.00pm was a special time for us to recite the Chaplet of Divine Mercy.

At this stage, all I could do for Liz was moisten her mouth with a swab, and pray by her side. I realised what Our Lady had meant by *"the little things you can do for Liz."*

One of Liz's favourite prayers was the Rosary. She was too weak to respond to conversation, but as I recited the Rosary she followed, her lips moving almost imperceptibly and her voice barely audible.

The Hail Mary was the last words on her lips.

Liz had no fear at all. I held her hand and promised her that I wouldn't let go until Seana took her other hand.

She left this world in peace and with joyful expectation at 3.30pm on December 18, 2008.

Reflection on Liz's Life

For a long time, I didn't always understand how Liz was so peaceful in her acceptance of all that befell her.

And in the end, she died as gently and peacefully as she lived.

Then I came across a reading from Saint Paul to the Corinthians while working on this chapter, and I don't believe it was a coincidence.

The words sum up everything most important in life and spirituality. It tells us how to behave toward our neighbours and fellow human beings.

And it describes Liz's virtues, more eloquently than anything I could ever write.

Liz was all about love, and so this message from Saint Paul could be describing her. These words sum up the essence of Liz for me:

"Love is patient and kind; love is not jealous or boastful; it is not arrogant or rude. Love does not insist on its own way; it is not irritable or resentful; it does not rejoice at wrong, but rejoices in the right. Love bears all things, believes all

things, hopes all things, endures all things. Love never ends... So faith, hope, love abide, these three; but the greatest of these is love."

Corinthians 13:4-8 & 13

One of the first pictures Liz ever bought is a framed excerpt of this quote from Saint Paul to the Corinthians. It hung in our first house and hung in every house since, including the one I live in now.

It reads: *"So faith, hope, love abide, these three; but the greatest of these is love."*

6

Last Stand for Liz

"And my God will meet all your needs according to the riches
of his glory in Christ Jesus."
Philippians 4:19

Nobody disturbed Liz and me for some time. I stayed by her side and didn't let go of her hand until P.J. came back from the chapel.

He didn't need to be told that she had passed. He said while he was down in the chapel, he felt a moment of peace that he never had before or since, and he knew Liz's soul was gone.

He said he waited in the chapel before he came up to give me some time with her.

P.J. alerted the nurses that Liz was gone, and they got a doctor to certify her death.

It was now well past 4.00pm. I felt physically and mentally drained, but still, things needed to be done.

I knew P.J. would go to our home in Rathvilly and bring back the suit that I wanted Liz buried in.

We contacted the funeral director in Portarlington, but he advised us that the mortuary staff had to release the body from the hospital.

They would be gone for the day by the time he'd get to Dublin; so it would be the next morning before they could collect Liz.

Hospital staff came to check if I was expecting many people to pay their respects to Liz. I explained that all her friends and family came to say goodbye when she was alive.

Then they said there was no hurry, but when I was ready, they would take Liz to the mortuary.

I hadn't thought about this before but instinctively, I knew Liz would hate to spend the night in a morgue.

She hadn't many fears in life, but being in a dark mortuary on her own? No, it wasn't happening.

"Liz isn't going to the mortuary," I said. They gently insisted Liz could not stay in the room.

I said I'd pay for the room. They still said she couldn't stay in the room because of infection control issues and health and safety issues.

"Well, she isn't going to the mortuary," I said.

I was determined about this. I could see the staff were doing their best to be kind, but I knew in my heart that Liz would never want to be left in a cold, dark morgue.

The hospital chaplain arrived offering any help or consolation that she could. So I asked her if we could move Liz to the hospital chapel for the night.

She was young and new to the job, and she looked a bit stunned.

"That wouldn't be standard practice here, and I don't have any authority to approve that," she said.

I asked her to try and find someone in charge of the hospital chapel and make my request to them. She looked very hesitant but said she would do what she could.

A while later, the nurses returned to remind me that we needed to move Liz to the mortuary.

They spoke about 'microbes' and 'best practice' and things I didn't really care about.

"*Well, can I spend the night with Liz in the mortuary then?*" I asked. They were adamant that I couldn't. Spending the night with her in the mortuary was definitely not possible.

"*Well then, Liz is not going to the mortuary either.*"

I wasn't rude or aggressive. I was too tired to even raise my voice. I was matter-of-fact and calm but resolved.

In the meantime, P.J. had pleaded with a funeral director who is a relation of ours and who knew Liz's family.

My brother wanted Liz to be taken to his house in Portarlington where we planned to wake her the next night.

The undertaker said his hands were legally tied because the hospital mortuary had to release Liz's body. He more or less told us that we were on our own until the next morning.

I knew the last thing in the world Liz would want was to spend the night in the morgue.

But I was torn because I also knew that she would hate me to disrupt the nursing staff and their terminally ill patients on her behalf.

Soon, the medical staff's pleas to move Liz were getting more urgent and more frequent.

I couldn't think straight anymore. I felt exhausted and stressed, but I was still determined not to give in. Liz was not going to the mortuary.

I prayed to Jesus to help me find a way.

Then at 8.00pm, my prayers were answered as Liz's angels of mercy flew in.

Niamh and Lorna had already heard the news of Liz's passing. They hugged me and kissed Liz and stroked her hair.

"*Don't worry, Sean, we're in charge now,*" said Lorna. "*You can spend the night here in this room with Liz, and we'll move her in the morning.*"

I would have cried with relief if I had any tears left to shed.

In the middle of all this, the girls only wanted to know if Seana came to take Liz's hand. I had to admit I didn't know, but I believed that she did.

More angels flew into Liz's hospital room shortly afterwards. Within minutes, Father John, the Catholic chaplain, arrived to offer a place off the chapel where I could spend the night with Liz.

There was yet another room beside it with a heater and tea and coffee facilities where P.J. could rest.

So that's where Liz and I spent our last night alone together.

God bless Niamh, Lorna and Father John.

By the way, Seana did come for Liz. I'm pretty sure she did.

7

Consolations Through Liz - I

"Ask, and it will be given to you; seek, and you will find;
knock, and the door will be opened to you."

Matthew 7:7

Saturday, December 20, 2008, the morning of Liz's funeral, was going to be the worst day of my life.

I felt lost and very alone without Liz. She was by my side and had been my best friend, companion and soulmate since I was a teenager.

Now I faced the awful prospect of life without her.

We'd been through so much together, even surviving the terrible losses of our children, Seana and Kieran.

And Liz had always said: *"Once we have one another, we can deal with whatever life throws at us."*

But we didn't have one another now, and I didn't know if I could deal with what life had thrown at me.

I didn't feel angry, and I tried not to question God's will during Liz's illness or in the immediate aftermath of her death.

I did, however, feel a sense of incredible desolation.

I prayed to Jesus in desperation. I needed help.

We waked Liz at P.J.'s and his wife, Joyce's house in Portarlington on the eve of the funeral, and I stayed there that night.

While Liz was dying, I had little or no sleep, and after her death, I had even less.

This ball of fear and sickening loneliness lodged in my chest, and it was impossible to sleep.

Sometime in the early hours of the morning, I must have dozed off from exhaustion.

Then as I woke, something incredible happened. Instead, of being crushed by the awful realisation that Liz was gone, the simplest details of our life flashed in front of my eyes, like a high-speed movie.

It was like having a panoramic view of our lives together. I saw all the joy, the peace, the laughter, the support, Liz's plan-B attitude, and all the unconditional love she showered on me.

I felt a sense of euphoria and realised how lucky and how incredibly fortunate I was to have shared my life with this woman for 42 years. I had a feeling of complete peace washing through me.

The experience lasted only minutes, but that sense of awe stayed with me the whole day of Liz's funeral. Instead, of having the worst day of my life, I thanked God for the great life we'd shared. I felt appreciation for the blessing of having her by my side for so long.

In the early years of our marriage, I was capable of being very angry and aggressive. I wouldn't talk about anything for long periods, and I drank too much.

Liz was a beautiful woman with a sunny and gentle disposition. She could have left me and found a better man, and no one would have blamed her for taking an easier path in life.

I know now I was fortunate that she stayed.

Part of my role as a priest now is to offer guidance to young couples preparing to get married. I warn them that almost 50% of the totality of all secular, common-law and sacramental marriages end in separation.

That could have been our fate, but I was lucky because Liz stuck by me.

I also recalled times when Liz and I tried to pick up the pieces of other people's broken and conflicted relationships.

We encountered a few bitter separations in our family. At work too, I got many unsolicited approaches from people troubled in their relationships.

People knew I had lost two children, and they hoped I had some magic formula to help them in their situations. I had to tell them that my magic formula was Liz.

But back then, and now as a priest, I see many people live lives that are purgatory on earth. Meanwhile, I had a taste of heaven on earth living with Liz.

The powerful consolation I received that morning, gave me the strength to get through Liz's funeral, a day that I'd been dreading.

That night, I decided to say the Rosary when I went to bed. The Rosary was the last experience that Liz and I shared, and I felt it would help me sleep or at least give me some peace of mind.

It did help, and after that, I said the Rosary every night, and I seldom felt alone again. I slept solidly again, and my nights became peaceful.

Each following morning for ten days in all, I experienced more consolations.

One day I woke to see what looked like a huge gold-coloured duvet in the sky. I understood it was a patchwork of events that constituted Liz's life.

It was filled with a dense material that dented as you pressed a fist or finger against it.

Liz had always seemed to have a great inner peace.

Yet, I was able to identify many fist-sized impressions as terrible losses in Liz's life.

As well as the heavy body blows, I also recognised some of my own fingerprint impressions left in the beautiful quilt. These were the youthful misdemeanours that I regretted.

Fortunately, there weren't many, and they weren't deep, so I understood that Liz had long forgiven me, which gave me further peace.

Within days, I faced into the first Christmas without Liz in more than four decades.

Our Lady's shrine at Knock was a favourite place, for Liz and me to visit whenever life got tough. We had planned to stay there that Christmas if Liz felt well enough to go.

I went on my own instead. Those early morning consolations managed to get me through the desolation and loneliness of that Christmas.

So instead of praying to Jesus for help to make it through the day, I started praying for a sign that Liz was okay.

"Jesus, let me know in a real and living way, that Liz is safe and well in your presence. I need to know that she is united with our children, parents, brothers and sisters, free from all pain, grief and fear and immersed in your compassion peace and love."

"If I know that, I'll be able to get up every morning, go to mass and continue to fulfil your will in this life in the best way I can."

On New Year's Eve, 13 days after Liz's death, I had dinner with my older sister, Pat. She lived close to P.J.'s house where I was still staying and had been a widow for five years.

We were both sad and trying to get through this festive occasion as best we could.

Early that evening we got a call from our younger sister May, in Bray in Wicklow, saying she needed to talk to me. She was breathless with excitement as she related her story.

She explained she left work at 6.00pm to get her hair done as she was going to a party later.

As she sat in her car outside the hairdressers finishing a cigarette, she found herself thinking of Liz.

She recalled looking up at the moon and wondering to herself *"Ah Liz, where are you now?"*

She said an incredible feeling of peace came over her, and she heard an internal voice that she recognised as Liz.

"She said that she was incredibly happy and united with Seana and Kieran, and she asked me to call you and let you know this. She wants you to know that they are watching over you."

May was only an occasional mass-goer and certainly not into mystical experiences. She would have been the last person I'd expect to get a message like this.

She said the powerful sense of peace she experienced stayed with her for weeks and continues to leave a lasting impression on her.

It was a better New Year's Eve than I ever imagined it could be.

Two months later, I joined a pilgrimage tour to San Giovanni in Italy to see Padre Pio. Liz and I have a devotion to Padre Pio since 1975.

Liz loved his simple advice: *"Pray, hope, and don't worry."*

Padre Pio had been exhumed the previous year, and his body was found incorrupt. His body was displayed in an open coffin for veneration at San Giovanni Rotondo.

The pilgrimage, which was peaceful and prayerful, was a success.

We spent our last night in Rome, to be close to the airport for return flight to Ireland the next morning.

Memories of Liz flooded back because the hotel was around the central Termini Station where we stayed a year earlier.

It was Liz's 60th birthday, and she wanted to mark the milestone by praying at the tomb of John Paul II in Rome. She was a huge admirer of John Paul.

Our tour group went to a mass that evening which was celebrated by an Irish priest based in Rome.

Everyone went on to a restaurant afterwards to celebrate our last night, but I wasn't in a celebratory mood.

I went back to our hotel for an early night. I was feeling more than a little sorry for myself.

At some stage during the night, I woke up to the sensation of a powerful presence in the room. It felt like Liz had swept in, even though I couldn't see or hear anyone.

I felt a sense of great peace again, and then I heard her words in my head: *"There's no need for you to feel so sad and lonely. The message I sent you, about how we are all here together and looking out for you is real."*

I lay there until the experience passed and then got up to see the time.

I looked at my watch and saw it had stopped with the hands on midnight. I went to my mobile phone to check the time but found the battery was dead.

I went back to sleep with a smile on my face.

I never went back to live in our home in Rathvilly because it had far too many memories of Liz.

I stayed with P.J. and Joyce and developed a routine which helped to fill my days.

Every morning I went to mass, and then I'd go back to the chapel at 3.00pm to say Divine Mercy Chaplet. Afterwards, I'd visit Liz and the children at the cemetery.

We had a headstone in place for Seana and Kieran, and all I needed to do was add Liz's name and dates to it. It's a lovely white marble headstone with pillars on either side of an angel, watching over the grave.

But I felt I needed an image of Liz, Seana and Kieran on the gravestone. I wanted to be able to focus on their lovely faces as I prayed.

The problem was that Liz liked simplicity and minimalism when it came to design. And all I could find were little oval shaped insets which held a single colour portrait.

I suspected she might think it gaudy to have three colour photos inserted on the gravestone.

I told P.J. and Joyce that I was torn between what I needed, and what Liz might want.

A month after being in Rome, I sat in my car outside the local church after finishing the Divine Mercy Chaplet. It was mid-afternoon, March 4, and it was Liz's birthday.

The weather was miserable. There was driving rain and howling wind around me. It was one of the wettest and wildest days I'd seen in a long time. I had my golf rain gear in the car as usual, but I felt low; I had no energy and continued sitting in the car.

The headstone was going through my head, worrying me, so I said:

"Liz, if you don't like what I'm planning to do with the headstone, you better let me know now because they'll be cutting the stone within days."

I was also at a loss what to do about getting a new home for myself.

I wanted to stay in Portarlington, but it was hard to muster any enthusiasm for house-hunting.

P.J. and Joyce gave me the use of a self-contained apartment off their house where I was free to stay as long as I liked. But I was aware that I had spent three months there at this stage.

"What am I going to do Liz? Where am I going to live?" I asked out loud.

Straight away, I got an impulse to drive to Pine Villa, a small housing estate on the outskirts of town.

Liz and I passed it years earlier when it was being developed.

We remarked that we'd like to live there if we ever returned to live in Portarlington.

I drove into the estate and saw a house with a 'for sale' sign outside. Then the rain cleared, so I drove back to the cemetery and followed my usual routine.

P.J. is a regular visitor to the cemetery too where all our loved ones are buried together.

Our parents, Jack and Mary Hyland's grave stands next to Liz's and the children's headstone.

Next to them is P.J.'s little girl Aine, who is Liz's and my godchild. She went to heaven in 1993 when she was only 4-years-old.

Over dinner on the night of Liz's birthday, P.J. said he saw an interesting headstone at the graveyard earlier.

He described it as a black marble plaque with a black and white portrait engraved or lasered into it like an etching.

He suggested it might be nicer than the ovals, so I said I'd look at it the next morning.

When I mentioned the house for sale in Pine Villa, P.J. said he knew the owner, and he'd sort out a viewing for me.

The next morning, I went to look at the plaque on the grave and knew this was what Liz wanted. The lovely image of Liz with our two babies on either side of her is now etched on black marble in the gravestone.

All Liz's family and anyone who knows Liz says this is exactly how she'd like it.

I went to look at the house in Pine Villa and never looked at another house after that.

It's now my home and where I enjoy great peace. I like to think that Liz sorted out the gravestone and my new home on her birthday that year.

Liz and I went on pilgrimages to Lourdes, Fatima, The Holy Land, Rome, Garabandal and The Divine Mercy Sites in Poland after the children died.

One of the few Marian shrines we hadn't visited was Medjugorje.

After Liz died, my youngest sister Kay, who suffers from bipolar depression, said she'd like to visit the pilgrimage town which is located in Bosnia and Herzegovina.

So, my sister Pat and I joined Kay for a trip to Medjugorje in April 2009.

Pat found it hard to accept the loss of her beloved husband, Derek when he died in 2003. They were a devoted couple, and she was deeply traumatised by his death.

She moved away from the Church and the sacraments for many years.

She told Kay and me that she wasn't interested in the pilgrimage aspect of our trip, and she was only there for the sun, scenery and experience.

Kay and I found the experience at Medjugorje both inspiring and moving.

Despite herself, it must have affected Pat too because when we returned to Ireland, she started going to daily mass.

Pat died without warning two months later in June 2009 when she was 62-years-old.

As a family, we were thankful that she had returned to the sacraments and was a daily mass-goer.

This was the grace of Medjugorje and the Blessed Virgin, for which I continue to give thanks.

Also, in June, I got a call from my former boss and work colleague, Lionel Alexander.

Lionel was part of the Hewlett Packard interview panel who hired me in 1995, and he was the managing director of their plant in Leixlip.

Lionel and Liz had a high regard for one another. He attended her funeral, but I hadn't spoken to him in the six months since that day.

We chatted for a while as he updated me on all the news at Hewlett Packard.

I noticed some hesitancy in his voice as he came around to the reason for his call.

"I'm not sure how you'll take this, but the real reason I'm calling is that I was asked to give you a message."

For a minute, I thought he meant a message from someone at Hewlett Packard.

"I feel a bit awkward because I'm not sure what you'll think," he continued. *"I had this dream where I met Liz, and she wants me to give you a message."*

Close up of portrait of Liz & children on the family headstone

Family Headstone

Liz's Memorial Card

Divine Mercy image used with permission of the Marians of the Immaculate Conception of the B.V.M

Liz's Memorial Card

Merciful Jesus, grant eternal rest to
the souls of the faithful departed.

SAFELY HOME

I am home in Heaven dear ones,
Oh! so happy and so bright,
There is perfect joy and beauty,
In this everlasting light.

All the pain and grief is over,
Every restless tossing passed,
I am now at peace forever,
Safely home in Heaven at last.

Did you wonder I so calmly,
Trod the valley of the shade?
Oh! but Jesus' love illumined,
Every dark and fearful glade.

And He came Himself to meet me,
In that way so hard to tread,
And with Jesus' arm to lean on,
Could I have one doubt or dread?

Then you must not grieve so sorely,
For I love you dearly still,
Try to look beyond earth's shadows,
Pray to trust our Father's will.

There is work still waiting for you,
So you must not idly stand;
Do it now while life remaineth,
You shall rest in Jesus' land.

When the work is all completed,
He will gently call you home,
Oh, the rapture of that meeting,
Oh, the joy to see you come.

Liz's Memorial Card

"Many have danced this dance called life.....but few with her gentle grace."

Together again.
You are in our hearts Always.

**Sacred Heart of Jesus
have mercy on the soul of
Liz Hyland**
Who died on 18th December, 2008.
Aged 61 years.
Rest in Peace.

8

Consolations Through Liz - II

"Blessed are those who mourn,
for they will be comforted."
Matthew 5:4

A message from Liz was the last thing I expected from my former boss. I could hardly breathe, but I begged Lionel to tell his story.

In this dream, he said was out for his usual morning run around his neighbourhood.

He recalled running along a familiar route and greeting his neighbours and friends. But then he took a turn, and he found himself on an unfamiliar road.

The road approached a large park with wrought iron railings. He could see a large crowd inside, who seemed to be attending some kind of festive occasion like a barbecue.

Then he saw Liz coming out of the park to approach him. He knew Liz was dead, but he said she came over to greet him with her beautiful, beaming smile as if nothing had happened.

"How are you, Lionel?" she asked.

"I'm fine," said Lionel. *"How are you, Liz?"*

"I'm good too, but I need you to give a message to John for me."

My birth cert and passport are in the name John, so everyone knew me as John in the work environment.

"Let him know how happy I am with Seana and Kieran, and let him know that we're watching over him, won't you Lionel?"

Liz turned to go back into the park, but Lionel said:

"Liz, I have to ask you one question, is there a heaven?"

He said she turned back and gave him one last radiant smile and said: *"Yes Lionel, there is."*

Then she turned and walked back into the park and disappeared into the crowds.

He admitted he was reluctant to tell me this because he wasn't sure how I'd feel about it. But the request was so explicit, and it felt so real, that he felt duty bound to tell me.

Of course, I wanted to know every last detail, so I met Lionel for lunch. After he repeated the story in detail, I asked if he could describe what Liz was wearing in the dream.

Lionel went on to describe what sounded like the very first dress I ever bought Liz in 1967.

It was during a time when I was working in Kerry for the ESB, and Liz worked in The Nationalist newspaper in Carlow in advertising and accounts.

She had an office dinner dance coming up, and there were no boutiques like you have now in the provincial towns.

No one even travelled to Dublin in those days to shop. Dublin seemed a world away then to country girls then.

I was driving through Limerick on the way home to Portarlington when I saw a boutique called Collette Modes. I had a good salary then, and I decided to surprise Liz buying her a new dress to wear to the dance.

The girl in the shop showed me a layered satin dress with a distinctive layer over one shoulder that hung like a shawl. It was cream with a very light brown print.

The dress Lionel described Liz as wearing had layers and a draped shawl, and was almost an exact description of that dress.

He could never have seen it because I don't even have a photo of Liz wearing it.

But I was a bit disappointed that he said the dress had a green print rather than brown. It fitted the description of the dress until then.

About six weeks later, two of Liz's best friends and members of Kilcock Golf Club came to visit me.

Ann Cribben and Eileen Foley were part of what they called 'Liz's gang' and were among those who visited her in her last days.

I told them about the messages from my sister May and Lionel. I mentioned that the dress that Liz wore was nearly the same as the one I bought her except the print Lionel saw was green rather than brown.

I tried to explain what the dress looked like and I pointed to Eileen's scarf because it was the same shade of brown as the print on the dress I bought Liz.

Eileen said: *"That's not brown, it's green."*

Ann and I thought it was brown, but Eileen was adamant it wasn't. That's when I knew Lionel had seen the very same dress that I bought.

Lionel's message from Liz gave me a tremendous sense of consolation and peace of mind.

I felt that my prayer, to know in a real and living way that Liz was safe and reunited with our children had been truly answered.

Liz and I often watched the Eternal Word Television Network - also known as EWTN.

She was a big fan of Mother Angelica the founder and presenter on this global Catholic TV network.

We also tuned into the news with Raymond Arroyo or programmes with the theologian, Scott Hahn.

I often watched evangelical preachers on other channels too as they're entertaining story-tellers when they interpret the Bible.

Some of them claim that the Bible says seventh heaven is 'a trillion, trillion miles away'. Or some huge number like that.

For some reason, that figure of 'a trillion, trillion miles' stuck in my head like a bad song that you can't forget. It made Liz and the children seem very far away.

I was sixty-one when Liz died, and my father, mother and uncles lived into their eighties. I knew there was a good chance I could live into my eighties too.

I didn't know how I'd be able to get up every day and walk this earth on my own for the next twenty years.

My prayers to Jesus now were of thanksgiving for the consolations and assurances I'd received about Liz. I was and will always be immeasurably grateful for these great consolations.

But now I added another prayer: *"Jesus, I'm so grateful for the consolations, but I don't know how to get up every day for possibly twenty years and keep going without Liz."*

"It seems too far in time and distance than I'm capable of coping with no matter how hard I try."

It went round and round in my head how far away Liz and the children were and how long it might be before I could see them again.

P.J. had a small cabin cruiser at a berth in Banagher in Offaly on the River Shannon. I joined him on the boat for the odd weekend to enjoy a change of scenery and to potter around.

He slept at one end of the boat, and I was at other in my own cabin.

I woke up there at 8.00am one weekend in July, but upon hearing P.J. snoring, I said my morning prayers rather than disturb him.

Out of nowhere, I was overwhelmed by a powerful sense of wellbeing, more powerful than anything I felt before.

I heard myself say: *"It's you Jesus...and Liz, Seana and Kieran are with you."*

Then I realised I could feel more spirits around me: *"Mam and Dad are here too."*

I can't say I saw anything or heard anything, but I felt it. I was transported into this all-embracing feeling of peace and wellbeing.

As the experience ebbed away, an internal voice said: *"Remember you didn't have to travel a trillion miles or wait twenty years. We are in your presence whenever you truly want us to be."*

I looked at my watch again, and it was about 8.30am.

I knew P.J. slept through it all because I could still hear him snoring. But I believed the feeling was so powerful, that he must have felt something on this little boat.

If he did, it would verify the experience I just had.

I was incredibly grateful for what I'd experienced but also felt ashamed because I always seemed to be doubting and looking for proof.

I felt like pointing towards P.J.'s room and say: *"It was him, Jesus, he wanted the proof."*

I didn't say anything to P.J. about what happened when he got up. We were out for a drive for a few hours, hardly exchanging a word, until we stopped for coffee.

Then P.J. said: *"You know, I had a lovely dream last night. I dreamt about Aine."*

His little girl Aine was born with an under-developed brain, and she could appear distressed at times.

"I seldom dream about her, but when I do, it's the way she used to be," explained P.J. *"But in the dream last night, she was running around.*

"She was laughing and happy with a big smile on her face. I could see Ma and Da in the background taking care of her. It was a lovely dream to have."

I asked if he had any idea about the time he had the dream.

"No, but I heard somewhere that the only dreams you can remember are the ones you have shortly before you wake up."

Only then did I tell him about my experience.

Once I got back to Portarlington, I went to the church and knelt in front of the tabernacle to give thanks for this incredible consolation.

I was so overcome with awe knowing that the Creator of this world, would take time to give me this consolation, that I broke down and cried.

That day, my prayer changed to: *"Jesus my life is yours, just let me know what you want me to do, and I'll try to do it."*

A Reflection on Consolations through Liz

Each of these wonderful consolations through Liz provided me with the comfort and reassurance I needed to get through my darkest time.

But there was much more to these experiences than that.

Throughout Jesus' time on earth, he preached the message that we should repent and be glad, for the Kingdom of God is close at hand.

Jesus wants us to understand that the Kingdom of God starts in our hearts right now.

Heaven is not somewhere up in outer space, where we will hopefully go in ten, twenty or thirty years' time. The Kingdom of God is within and all around us now, today.

What I really learnt from these experiences was the message: *"Remember you didn't have to travel a trillion miles or wait twenty years. We are in your presence whenever you truly want us to be."*

As a priest I'm called, like all priests, to provide support and consolation to people all the time.

We provide pastoral care to people who are grieving for lost loved ones, or worried about a sick loved one. We deal with people suffering from all sorts of problems including mental, physical, financial and spiritual afflictions.

Sometimes, if I think it'll help, I'll share the experience of my consolations of faith with people.

Often, I discover that they've had these kinds of experiences themselves.

Many older people, in particular, will remember a spiritual experience that they put out of their minds. They never discussed it with anybody in case people thought they were losing their minds.

They wonder if they had, in fact, imagined the experience or dreamt it. Yet, they still remember it vividly.

I've discovered that many people, more than we ever hear of, receive consolations. Two books by the author Colm Keane, Going Home and the Distant Shore, document hundreds of these types of experiences.

Then there are the people who don't receive these consolations but need them. I often try to help these people to be more open to receiving these types of consolations.

I use the television in the corner of the room as an example. If it's not plugged in, it's a square piece of furniture with a glass pane in the front.

Even if it's plugged in, but isn't tuned to a station, all we'll see is random flickers of static 'snow' and a sound of buzzing noise.

It's only when the TV is plugged in and tuned in, that you can see and hear what's happening in every corner of the world.

Many of us are disconnected from the Kingdom of God in our daily lives. We're distracted by the noise of this world and our material desires.

Even those of us who call ourselves Christians can be like the disconnected television. We have all the working parts to receive a signal, but we're not plugged in.

Some of us are plugged in, but not tuned in. We believe in God, say a few prayers, go to Mass every Sunday and live blameless lives.

We sometimes feel God's grace trying to break through, to give us the consolation we're seeking. But we're not tuned in, so all we receive is static snow and buzzing noise.

What I've learnt is that God's help and consolation are here for those who want it. He's not in a very faraway place, a trillion miles from here; He is here with us now.

And Jesus said: *"Ask, and it will be given to you; seek, and you will find; knock, and the door will be opened to you."*

There's an ancient song from the indigenous people of Peru that explains disconnection from God better than I can.

God is With Us

A man whispered: "God speak to me."
And a bird began to sing.
But the man did not hear.

Then the man repeated: "God speak to me."
And the echo of thunder was heard.
But the man was unable to hear.
Then he looked around and said: "God let me see you."
And a star shone on the heavens.
But the man did not see it.

The man began to shout: "God show me a miracle."
And a baby was born.
But the man did not feel the heartbeat of life.

Then the man became desperate and cried:
"God touch me and assure me you are with me."

And a butterfly alighted gently on his shoulder.
The man brushed off the butterfly with his hand.

And disillusioned, he continued on his way,
Sad, alone and afraid.

9
Christmas in the Holy Land

"And she gave birth to her firstborn, a son. She wrapped him in cloths and placed him in a manger because there was no guest room available for them. And there were shepherds living out in the fields nearby, keeping watch over their flocks at night. An angel of the Lord appeared to them, and the glory of the Lord shone around them, and they were terrified. But the angel said to them, "Do not be afraid. I bring you good news that will cause great joy for all the people. Today in the town of David a Saviour has been born to you; He is the Messiah, the Lord."
Luke 2:7-11

Let me jump forward to November 2009, as I faced into Liz's first anniversary and my second Christmas without her.

By then I was exploring the prospect of entering the priesthood and studying philosophy and theology in St Patrick's College in Carlow.

I'll relate that journey in full in the next chapter.

Meanwhile, the previous months had flown by in a whirl of emotions, decisions and studies.

Then one day I looked at the calendar and realised that it was November, the month before Christmas, and I had no plans made.

We spent three weeks in the Algarve in Portugal for Liz's last Christmas. We'd never spent that much time away before, but it was my first Christmas as a retiree.

Yet Liz seemed tired towards the end of the three weeks, and I thought she might have been overdoing the golf.

"What if we take a shorter break next year and we go to the Holy Land next Christmas?" I suggested.

We had been on a parish pilgrimage tour to the Holy Land twenty-five years earlier and had seen many of the sights.

"Think of it, we could celebrate midnight mass on Christmas Eve in Bethlehem, and then we could take it easy."

"I'd love that, Sean," said Liz. *"We have all year to organise it in time too."*

It turned out that we didn't have all year. We shelved the idea of the Holy Land once Liz was diagnosed with cancer in April.

A few months later, we said we'd go to Knock instead, but Liz was in heaven the week before Christmas. I ended up in Knock alone.

Now that Christmas was looming again, I decided the place I most wanted to be on earth was in the Holy Land.

I needed to celebrate Christmas Eve at midnight mass in Bethlehem for both Liz and me. It would make me feel closer to Liz again.

I must have phoned most the travel agents in Ireland, but I hit a brick wall.

No, they said, there are no tours to the Holy Land over Christmas.

I felt defeated. I didn't have the energy to research and arrange the trip independently, so it looked like I'd be returning to Knock again.

During a break in college, I checked online for availability in Knock over Christmas and discovered there was only one hotel open in December, and it was almost booked out.

I turned the key in my front door fully intending to book the hotel straight away, but instead picked up a flyer dropped in by a local travel consultant.

The flyer said she was newly appointed as an agent for a UK travel company that specialised in customised trips worldwide.

"There's no harm in trying!" I said, so I phoned the number on the flyer in a last-ditch bid to get to the Holy Land for Christmas.

It turned out the travel agent lived a few doors from me in my estate, and better still, she could get me to Bethlehem or near it.

She said she had a nine-day tour of Israel starting in Jerusalem on Christmas day. The others on the trip were American-Israelis visiting their homeland.

I explained how I wanted to attend midnight mass on Christmas Eve in Bethlehem and asked if she could get me there a few days earlier.

There was no problem getting me to Jerusalem early, but that's when things got a little more complicated.

She explained they couldn't arrange a tour to Bethlehem, because it's a Palestinian town and Israeli guides are not allowed for security reasons.

She also warned that the midnight service on Christmas Eve in St Catherine's in Bethlehem was by ticket and invitation only.

Palestinian President, Mahmoud Abbas was attending the mass, and security would be tight, so there was little chance of getting in.

I booked the trip anyway. I felt optimistic that I'd find my way to Bethlehem and celebrate midnight mass there on Christmas Eve.

I arrived at my hotel in Jerusalem at 6.00am on the morning of December 24 and asked the concierge to find a tour for Bethlehem that night.

He didn't know if he could find a space at short notice, but he said there was no possibility of getting into the mass.

"Sir, at best, you can get into Manger Square outside the church, and you can watch the mass being broadcast on big screens," he said.

He succeeded in finding me a place on a tour with a Palestinian guide that night.

Of course, our first stop in Palestine was a souvenir shop, where I bought a pack of ten prayer cards.

These little cards had pressed flowers and an image of the nativity scene, and they were printed with the message: *'I have prayed for you in Bethlehem.'*

We arrived at 10.00pm in ancient Manger Square, an area which can hold up to 70,000 people.

We stood outside St Catherine's and adjoining Basilica of the Nativity below it. The English mass in St. Catherine's is broadcast around the world on Christmas Eve.

The actual spot where Jesus was born is located in the small Nativity church next door. It's located down a flight of stairs under the altar in a crypt called the Grotto of the Nativity.

I didn't appreciate how difficult it would be to get into the churches until I saw they were fenced off and manned by Palestinian soldiers with AK47s.

Our chances of getting into either church looked unlikely.

Our tour guide said he would do his best to get us nearer the church, so we stood for an hour in the square listening to hymns being broadcast from St Catherine's.

There was no sign of the big screens working, and the crowd grew bigger and more restless.

Our guide appeared to have a brother or cousin in the Palestinian security detail because suddenly, he made an urgent gesture to follow him.

A security barrier opened and closed again behind us, and we found ourselves in a small courtyard in front of the Church of the Nativity.

We were now in a group of about 150 people standing outside the Church of the Nativity door which was manned by more Palestinian soldiers.

The crowd was waiting to pay homage at Jesus's birthplace after midnight mass ended.

Not knowing how long we'd be waiting, I sat on the edge of a large concrete plant container until I noticed a local woman on crutches.

I offered the woman my seat instead. Her daughter went up to the guards and pointed at her elderly mother's crutches. Then the guards beckoned to the old lady and me to come into the church.

They assumed that I was with the two women because I was talking to them.

So, in minutes I'd left my tour group behind, and I found myself in the Church of the Nativity on Christmas Eve.

I felt so grateful to be there.

I looked down the small spiral staircase that led into the Grotto of the Nativity, the actual place where Jesus was born.

Christmas Eve mass in the grotto was for the privileged few and most likely being celebrated by a bishop with connections to the custodians of the crypt.

I could see there were many people assembled down there already. It was strictly private and invite only, and I didn't have an invite.

And then I spotted an old woman wearing a black shawl gesturing at me to come down and join them.

Maybe I was gazing down those stairs so longingly that the old lady took pity on me. I don't know the reason.

I don't even know who she was apart from being an angel, and I didn't question her.

I picked my way down those spiral steps as fast as I could and managed to squeeze through the crowd into this intimate space.

When my eyes adjusted to the light, I realised I was standing right beside the Grotto of the Manger.

This is the exact spot where Mary laid her new-born Son and where they place a crib for the two weeks of Christmas.

I stood looking in awe at the spot that Jesus was born 2,009 years earlier. I made sure that Liz's memorial card and my ten prayer cards touched the crib during the mass.

And I cried in thanksgiving to be celebrating mass at the same time and exact place of Jesus' birth.

I was incredibly moved by the mass, and I knew it was no accident I was there.

I felt a great sense of closeness to Liz, Seana and Kieran.

On Christmas day, I joined the American-Israeli group for my nine-day tour as scheduled.

Our tour brought us to the Old City where we visited the Church of the Holy Sepulchre.

This cathedral was built on the site of Calvary where Jesus was crucified, and it also contains the Sepulchre or Jesus's empty tomb.

Pilgrims flock to Jerusalem at Christmas, so we spent about an hour queuing to see the holy site.

By now the guide estimated there was a two-hour queue to get up the narrow flight of stairs to see Calvary.

"We have to get to The Garden of Gethsemane before it closes," said the guide. "So sorry, but we've no time to queue for Calvary."

He suggested we could return privately on our last free day on Sunday.

I was the only one who returned to Calvary as the rest of the group wanted to go to Bethlehem that day.

I got into the Chapel of the Crucifixion at 11.30am and saw vast numbers of pilgrims queuing to touch the rock of Calvary located on the floor of the altar.

I hoped to be able to say my Divine Mercy Chaplet in front of the altar on the hour of Christ's death at 3.00pm.

I found some seats about twenty feet away from the altar and sat waiting there. I timed the movement of the queue and planned to re-join it so I could be in front of Calvary on the appointed hour.

But at around at 2.30pm, as I was getting ready to re-join the big line of pilgrims, a monk pushed back the queue. He roped off the entire area in front of Calvary including the seats I sat on.

I sat twenty feet away from the Chapel of the Crucifixion altar and Calvary with not a single person in front of me.

The Monk paid no attention to me. Nor did the Eastern Orthodox priest who came out and waved incense in front of the altar. When he finished a Franciscan Priest came out and did the same.

I said my prayers with my perfect view of Calvary until after 3.00pm.

All I could say was: *"Thank you, Jesus."*

It felt as if Jesus was saying: *"You want to say the Divine Mercy Chaplet in front of Calvary at 3.00pm? You've got it."*

My tour group visited more sites like the Dead Sea, the Masada fortress, the Sea of Galilee, Capernaum and Nazareth.

We also went to the Church of The Annunciation in Nazareth.

Below it is the Grotto of the Annunciation, which holds the remains of the childhood home of Mary and the place of the Annunciation.

Again, the queue to file past this grotto was too long, and my tour group moved on. I let the guide know I'd catch up with him.

I was keeping an eye on my watch and getting my camera ready to take a photo when I found myself at the grotto.

I'd been fussing so much that I forgot to think about a prayer.

At that precise second, the bells for noontime devotion rang out and prompted me to start saying the Angelus.

It felt as if the Blessed Virgin was saying to me: *"Don't worry, I'll tell you what prayer to say."*

To me, it was the Holy Land welcomed me with open arms.

Thinking back, the good omens started in Dublin airport even before I boarded the plane to Israel.

That day, I nipped into the airport chapel to say The Divine Mercy Chaplet.

It was the day before Christmas Eve, and a couple of ladies were setting up the altar.

The church has a four-foot high image of the Divine Mercy beside the altar. It stood beside a small Christmas tree with twinkling white lights.

While reciting the prayers, I saw the Divine Mercy image become bathed in a soothing purple glow. I admired the lovely light effect, but it disappeared before I finished.

I wondered how it was done, so I checked the base of the tree expecting to see a spotlight on a timer. I couldn't see anything there.

The ladies were passing back and forward from the Sacristy so, I thought they must have switched the light on and off in there.

As I sat down again to say a final prayer before leaving, a priest came in and apologised for all the disruption.

I complimented him on the beautiful light effects he had for the Divine Mercy Image.

He looked at me quizzically and assured me there was no light.

I felt he was thinking: *"Ah well, it's Christmas. What harm if he has a drink or two on him?"*

That purple glow on The Divine Mercy image was just part of the pattern of signs and consolations I experienced on that trip.

It was a wonderful pilgrimage, and I had no doubt that Liz, Seana and Kieran were close by me all through Christmas.

Testimonies of Healings

Before leaving Dublin Airport, I got a text saying that Liz's nephew T.J. and his wife, Louise, had given birth to a premature baby, Eve.

I prayed for Louise and Eve by the manger during Christmas Eve Mass in Bethlehem.

As soon as I got home, I gave Louise one of the prayer cards that touched the crib at that special Mass.

Healing Testimony from Louise

On December 21, 2009, our daughter Eve was born at 27 weeks weighing 940g or 2lbs. She was very fragile and so small.

A family member contacted Sean to inform him about Eve's birth. On Sean's journey to Bethlehem, he included Eve and myself in his prayers.

On his return home, he gave Eve a card with flowers from Bethlehem which is very precious to us.

This card touched the spot of the manger at midnight Mass on Christmas Eve, 2009.

We attached the card to Eve's hospital incubator, and somehow, we had a sense that Eve was going to improve and come home safe to us.

Eve struggled with her oxygen levels and needed a blood transfusion but gained weight and got stronger day by day.

She has met all her milestones, and is now a very happy and healthy child.

I have always said that "Eve was never on her own, in that incubator."

All the extra help and support and prayers helped her home to us.

I gave out the rest of the cards to Liz's and my brothers and sisters and had just one Bethlehem prayer card left.

Then in 2010, I met a friend of my late sister Pat's called Collette.

She told me about her niece who was pregnant and struggling after a tragic sequence of events.

I gave her the last Bethlehem prayer card I had.

I prayed to Jesus to provide a healing blessing and consolation of faith for Collette's niece, Margaret Foyne.

Here is Margaret's account of the events that followed.

Healing Testimony from Margaret

We were trying for another baby for years, and after many miscarriages, you can only imagine the joy when we found out we were expecting twins.

Sadly, early in the pregnancy one twin died, and we knew the other baby was struggling to survive.

In 2010, at 19 weeks pregnant, we got news that our baby had several abnormalities.

They told us she probably wouldn't be born alive and if she was, they wouldn't be able to operate on her as her heart was not developed properly.

The following Monday my husband took his own life.

It was a devastating time on top of what we already had to deal with. My family and friends helped my children and me through it.

We were in everyone's prayers.

My aunt Colette gave me a relic which she received from Father Seán and from that week on, the diagnosis for our baby improved.

I also believe that the prayers of hundreds of people helped.

Róise was born a perfect baby girl on November 17, 2010. She was very small at 4lbs 13oz, but her heart was normal.

We went from buying a little blanket to bury her in, to having the outgoing, wonderful, loving young girl we have today.

She lights up all our lives and our home.

Thank you, Father Seán for the Relic from Bethlehem; we are forever grateful.

Regards

Margaret

The good news continues as Margaret has since remarried, and both Róise and Eve are doing well today.

And I will never, ever forget the experience of midnight Mass in Bethlehem, and until the day I die and after, I will always be eternally grateful to Our Lord for that consolation of faith.

Return Visit to the Holy Land

I heard about a pilgrimage to the Holy Land during an overnight workshop for priests in early 2017.

The parish priest of Tullow, Father Andy Leahy and Monsignor Brendan Byrne said they were organising a trip in October 2017.

I told them my memories of the Holy Land in Christmas 2009 and said I'd love to join them on their trip.

It was a small group of twenty people, and many of them were nieces and family of Monsignor Byrne.

Father Andy was the group leader, and he organised a rota so that we'd take turns celebrating mass for the group.

On our second morning in the Holy Land, we set out for Bethlehem.

We planned to celebrate mass in the cell where Saint Jerome, at the request of the Pope, spent years translating the New Testament from its original language of Greek and Hebrew into Latin.

Saint Jerome's cell adjoins the site venerated as the birthplace of Jesus. Just a wall separated us from the Grotto of the Nativity.

Father Andy remembered my utter joy at the memory of attending midnight mass in Bethlehem years earlier. So he kindly invited me to celebrate the mass that morning. I treasured the privilege.

The bus trip from our hotel in Jerusalem to Bethlehem took about thirty minutes.

I took the microphone on the bus on the way out and related the story of attending midnight mass in Bethlehem at Christmas 2009.

As we walked to Saint Jerome's cell for mass, I was able to point out where I was standing in Manger Square and where I went until I found myself touching the Manger on Christmas Eve.

I celebrated mass with my back almost touching the wall which separated us from the Manger.

It was one of the most cherished masses I've celebrated since becoming a priest.

Again as we travelled on the bus to Calvary, I used the bus microphone to share my experience at Calvary in 2009, and likewise at the Church of the Annunciation in Nazareth.

It was an enormous privilege for me to return to these holy places as a priest and celebrate mass. It was another of my many blessings from heaven.

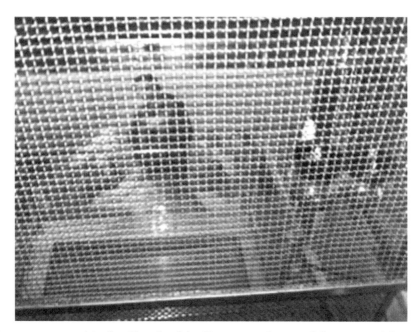

The spot venerated in the Church of the Nativity as the site of the manger. The crib is placed in the manger area over Christmas

Calvary

Calvary

Grotto of the Annunciation

10

Call to the Priesthood

"For the gifts and the calling of God are irrevocable."
Romans 11:29

The days seemed to grow longer after Liz died.

I had my routine of attending mass in the morning, then returning to the church at 3.00pm for the Divine Mercy Chaplet and afterwards on to the cemetery.

I joined the golf club in Portarlington and played with the seniors two days a week.

I was also invited to join a wonderful prayer group by a friend of my late sister Pat called Collette. It's called Teach Mhuire and has been going for many years.

They meet once a week to read some scripture, pray and sing hymns in praise of God. I went there every Tuesday evening. It was a wonderful support in that first year after Liz's death.

I still wanted to do something in thanksgiving for the incredible consolations I had received.

I thought about volunteering for a charity like Saint Vincent de Paul or meals on wheels for the elderly. I prayed to Jesus and told him I would do his will.

In May, I read an article in the Irish Catholic promoting vocations to the priesthood, which included profiles of seminarians at Saint Patrick's College in Maynooth.

Among them, was a mature student in his early sixties with a grown-up family. He lost his wife through cancer a couple of years earlier and was now in his first year at Maynooth.

I recall saying: *"Jesus, I know I said I'd do your will but I was thinking of a bit of charity work. I'm not thinking along these lines at all."*

I'd never even considered the priesthood before, but now the idea wouldn't go away.

I decided to contact the mature student in the Irish Catholic, and he agreed to meet with me.

I recall driving to Maynooth and saying: *"Jesus, you and I know this is not going to go anywhere. But I'll go where you seem to be guiding me, and please point me towards what you really want me to do."*

I met with the man with the late vocation. He was very committed, but he made it clear that it was difficult being a seminarian in your sixties.

Returning to study and academic life, living in a community and completing the tough formation programme is not for everyone.

I didn't like the sound of it at all.

I breathed a sigh of relief as I drove home. I learnt enough to know that was not the route for me.

I felt too old and too emotionally fragile to take on anything as demanding as that. I could barely handle my own little daily routine as it was.

I put the idea of the priesthood to one side, relieved that this was not the path Jesus was pointing me towards. I wondered if I should explore another avenue like becoming a permanent deacon or a lay minister.

"Thank you, Jesus," I said. *"I can see the priesthood is not the path for me."*

However, I was the only one doing the talking.

In June, I heard the National Charismatic Conference was taking place in Athlone Regional College.

Liz and I had never been part of the Catholic Charismatic thing.

We went to meetings in the eighties, but all the healings, speaking in tongues and uplifted hands were too expressive for us.

But I went to the conference anyway, because I feel that the Holy Spirit does appear in a unique way in the Charismatic movement.

I stayed in student accommodation sharing an apartment with a family man, Noel Healy, from Limerick.

Like me, he was there to learn more about the Charismatic movement.

He went to Medjugorje years earlier and found it such an emotional experience that it inspired him to get closer to Jesus.

I told him I was looking for a new path since my wife died. I explained I'd spoken with a mature seminarian in Maynooth but ruled out studying for the priesthood.

Noel, who now runs the Padre Pio Healing Rooms in Kilkee, County Clare, insisted that I shouldn't rule the priesthood out until I explored it more.

He suggested meeting a friend of his Father Fred MacDonnell, a curate in Meelick in Limerick.

"He has a grown family and lost his wife through cancer shortly after he retired to too," he said.

"He studied for the priesthood at the Beda Pontifical College in Rome, and he's never regretted that decision. You should meet him and talk to him too."

Noel explained that the Beda College in Rome is a seminary for mature students with all courses conducted in English. They have a shorter four-year programme to ordination.

I still didn't feel that the priesthood was for me, so I wasn't optimistic that it would lead anywhere.

But I met Father Fred and spent a couple of hours talking to him. I heard how he worked as a bus inspector in C.I.E., raised a family of five with his wife Ann and had a calling to the priesthood when she died.

I loved his enthusiasm for his job, and I could see how he loved ministering to parishioners. He was very encouraging about the whole seminary training too.

When ordained in Saint John's Cathedral in Limerick in 2003, he was 69-years-old.

He said he wanted to serve for at least 10 years as a priest.

His wish was granted when he passed away at the end of 2013 just before his 80th birthday.

After meeting with Father Fred in 2009, I felt lighter and inspired.

On the drive home, I said: *"Jesus, if this is what you really want me to do, I think I could do it."*

Once I approached my parish priest Father Tom Dooley about a late vocation, things started to move quickly.

He talked to Bishop Jim Moriarty who set up an appointment with the diocesan vocations director, Father Ruairi O Domhnaill.

The vetting process went smoothly, and I was approved to study for the priesthood by late September.

By this time, it was too late to start in the seminary that year.

They suggested I study modules in philosophy and theology as part of a Humanities degree course in St Patrick's College, Carlow.

It was a good way to see how I'd cope with returning to academic studies, and it gave me plenty of space to reconsider the path I was taking.

I enjoyed being in college three mornings a week, and the idea of joining the priesthood had plenty of time to percolate.

By the following year, I looked forward to going into a seminary, and I had no doubts about my vocation any more.

My biggest dilemma was choosing whether to go to Maynooth or to the Beda in Rome in September 2010.

There were pros and cons to either option.

The advantage of Maynooth was I could get home every weekend to visit the cemetery, play a round of golf and see my friends and family.

The disadvantage was it's a six-year programme with no credit for life experience, academic achievements or maturity.

Everyone told me that the Beda was more suitable for a mature vocation.

But my greatest concern with going to Rome was not being able to visit the cemetery.

I was used to visiting the graves every day since Liz died, and I knew I'd miss the sense of peace and consolation I got from those visits.

I felt this daily routine helped me to stay sane.

I worried too how would Liz feel if I went to Rome and only visited a couple of times per year.

Father Ruairi O'Domhnaill, the vocations director, kindly reserved a place in both locations to give me more time to decide.

I discovered that the mature seminarian in Maynooth, who I spoke with the year before, had already quit. That was further confirmation that Rome might be the better prospect for a mature vocation like mine.

But I wrestled with the decision all summer.

As I related earlier, I went to Medjugorje for the first time ever in Easter 2009 with my two sisters Pat and Kay.

I went again in Easter 2010 with Kay and Liz's sister, Margaret for a second peaceful and prayerful pilgrimage.

When the Teach Mhuire prayer group arranged a pilgrimage to Medjugorje in August 2010, I decided to go again.

This time I prayed that Jesus through his Blessed Mother and Liz would help me decide if I should go to Maynooth or Rome for the priesthood.

By now, I felt that Rome was the better path for me, but I didn't have any idea how Liz would feel about this. I wanted her support and guidance.

So, I said: *"Liz, it looks like I'll be heading to Rome in late September unless you let me know you prefer Maynooth."*

August 25 was the second last day of the pilgrimage and is the day the Blessed Virgin gives her monthly message to the visionaries.

Once again, I enjoyed the sense of peace, light and love that exists in Medjugorje. But I was going home the following day, and I still had no idea what Liz wanted.

It's scorching in Medjugorje in August so, like most people, I climbed the hills to the prayer spots in the early morning or late evening. Then I spent the middle of the day in the two churches in the town.

The Rosary is said every evening in Saint James' Church, with a few minutes silence held at the time Our Lady appears to the visionaries.

The visionaries are not usually present, but the church fills to capacity on this day every month.

Even though the town is full of reverence and love, there's a little hostility towards Italian pilgrims.

They're the largest nationality of pilgrims in Medjugorje as Italy is only a short boat trip away. Many are loud and expressive, and they're accused of blocking all the roads with their camper vans and tour buses.

The townspeople complain they don't contribute to the economy in the area as they don't use local hotels or taxis.

Pilgrims complain that they have their own Italian language masses, but they barge into other masses leaving no room for anyone else.

Monitors are even placed at the church doors to discourage this from happening.

This was my third time in Medjugorje, and I had my favourite positions in the churches.

I liked to sit in the centre of Saint James' Church where I had a view of the Tabernacle and a statue of the Blessed Virgin.

The numbers of supporting pillars in the church mean that a view of one or the other is often blocked in other parts of the church.

I entered the church long before the Rosary started so it was still empty and quiet.

I stepped past a man, into a seat to sit in my usual spot. He started to wave his arms and talked animatedly in Italian.

He pointed to scarves he had placed along the seat indicating that he had reserved the seating for about ten people.

I paused for a second, and then probably prejudiced by the complaints I'd heard about Italians, I decided to ignore him.

I thought: *"This is crazy reserving ten seats a quarter hour before the Rosary begins in a half-empty church."*

So, I blanked his protestations, pushed aside a few of his scarves and sat down.

As more and more people started filling the seats, I gathered my thoughts to say my prayers.

Instead, I received an internal message, and the words were unequivocal: *"We do not do things like that."*

I felt so ashamed; like a small boy who has been justly chastised. I knew it had to be Liz ensuring that I don't slip back into my old aggressive habits.

I stayed kneeling for a while trying to decide what to do.

I knew I had to leave the seat and apologise to the Italian pilgrim, both of which I did. The Rosary was about to start, and the church was now full of people standing in the aisles.

I found a spot to kneel on in front of the altar rails along with many other people.

I placed Liz's memory card on the floor in front of me. During the moment of silence, I glanced down at the memory card and Liz's name completely dominated the card.

The lettering of Liz's name was five or six times its usual size, and I felt a wonderful sense of wellbeing again.

I travelled home the next day confident that Liz had communicated with me.

It reassured me that she's still keeping an eye on me, and she seemed to let me know she supported my decision to go to Rome.

My first evening back in Ireland, my sister May phoned me to say she had another amazing communication from Liz.

May worked as a nurse in a department in St John of God's in Shankill providing day care for elderly people.

She was attending Eucharistic Adoration at the centre, and as she prayed, she gazed into a garden outside.

Suddenly, May felt transported into another more beautiful garden setting, and Liz was standing before her smiling the most radiant smile she'd ever seen.

May was scared of death until then, but since seeing Liz's smile, she says she no longer worries about dying.

Liz was only present for an instant and didn't speak, but May was amazed at how vivid and real-life it felt. She said the vision wasn't hazy, vague or one-dimensional.

But she admitted that one or two things about Liz's appearance that bothered her. She said Liz looked different because her hair looked very black in her apparition.

May lived in England for many years, so she didn't get to know Liz until she returned to Ireland in the Eighties.

I reassured her that Liz's hair was naturally black, but as she aged, she coloured it, and her hair drifted to lighter shades of brown and auburn.

May also thought that the vision was odd because Liz appeared to her wearing a very short mini skirt.

She had only seen Liz in the stylish but conventional and modest wardrobe of her older years.

I laughed thinking of Liz in the sixties and early seventies when she always wore mini-skirts.

May described Liz wearing a red fitted jacket and matching red mini-skirt.

I knew from her description that this was the second outfit I bought for Liz in Limerick in 1968.

Liz loved it so much that she even brought it on honeymoon a few years later to Spain.

We had a photo of her wearing the suit outside our hotel in the seventies, so I dug it out and brought it to May the next day.

She said, without doubt, it was the exact suit Liz was wearing.

She said the only difference between the photo and her vision was Liz's smile. In our picture, Liz isn't smiling for once.

May said her radiant and glowing smile was the most striking aspect of the vision she had.

When we worked out the time of May's vision on August 25, it was when I was in the chapel in Medjugorje.

It was also the first time that I began to feel at peace with the decision to go to Rome.

I knew Liz's smile meant for certain that she was happy with me going to Rome.

On reflection, there was another message Liz communicated in this vision and it may have been something to do with a gift that my older sister Pat gave to me.

The week before she died, Pat asked what I missed most about Liz. I immediately said it was her smile.

I told Pat, that when I arrived home from work during the darkest days of our grieving after losing the children, Liz would still greet me with that beautiful smile.

It was a smile that said: "In spite of the enormous pain I'm feeling, I'm so glad to see you, and I want to help ease your pain."

At the time I didn't appreciate how much that smile cost her, but as the years rolled on, I've realised how strong and brave she was.

The loss of two children would have broken many people, and without Liz, it might have broken me.

Days before Pat died, she gave me a gift of a plaque I'll always treasure called Her Smile.

Her Smile

Though her smile is gone forever,
and her hand I cannot touch,
I still have so many memories,
of the one I loved so much.

Her memory is my keepsake,
with which I'll never part.
God has her in His keeping.
I have her in my heart.

May says she doesn't have words to describe how beautiful Liz's smile was, and I envy her because she was the one to see it.

But I know it was Liz's way of letting me know again that she's watching over me and supporting me on every step of my journey.

I only ever bought Liz three outfits in all our years together. Once I realised how style conscious she was, I was afraid to even buy a scarf for her on my own.

She has appeared to Lionel and May in the first two outfits, but there is one left.

One of my dearest wishes is that Liz will visit me wearing her grey trouser suit before I die. As you can imagine, I'm hoping it'll be soon.

Liz's smile - more like the one May described

Liz in her red suit

11

Seminary Life

"I will study your commandments and reflect on your ways.
I will delight in your decrees and not forget your word."
Psalm 119:15-16

As I boarded the plane for Rome to begin my studies for the priesthood, all my confidence about my vocation fled.

At age 63, I was retired now for four years and faced the prospect of getting back to serious studies. Doing a few hours a week in philosophy and theology in St Patrick's College in Carlow was manageable. But I felt nervous about doing this full-time.

I wasn't confident about being a student. In my schooldays, I was never the studious type or anywhere near the top of the class.

The prospect of being away from the cemetery for long periods worried me too. I got a lot of comfort from prayer and meditation at Liz and the children's graves.

Sometimes I thought those hours in the cemetery were the only thing keeping me sane. I wondered how I would cope without being there.

Also, I dreaded living in a close community with a lot of strangers.

I had only lived with Liz for the past four decades, and we enjoyed a lot of freedom. We lived our lives in a way that suited ourselves.

I feared I wouldn't be able to handle moving into a community with its rules, regulations and structures. I thought that living in a seminary might be too confining and oppressive.

The old saying *"You can't teach an old dog new tricks"* was going around in my head a lot.

As I flew to Rome that day in September 2010, I wondered would I be returning as fast. There seemed to be a lot of insurmountable hurdles. If one of these concerns didn't cause me to quit, the other might.

My words to Jesus were: *"You and I know this is probably not going to work, but you won't be able to say I didn't try."*

The Pontifical Beda College, to give it its full title, was founded in 1852 with the aim of training older men for the Catholic priesthood. It has always been one of the smaller seminaries and is run by the Bishops of England and Wales.

The college stands across from the Basilica of Saint Paul Outside the Walls. *'Outside the Walls'* means precisely what it says - the Basilica and the Beda are located immediately outside the walls of Vatican City.

The Beda occupies a building built in the 60s and apart from its lovely garden, it looks like any anonymous three-star hotel. It's a four-storey tall, rectangular block set among some beautiful historic buildings.

The Beda training is four years long, as opposed to the traditional seven years. Older candidates are fast-tracked to the priesthood because we're seen as having already acquired significant life skills and experience.

Successful students get a degree in theology and philosophy at the end of year three, and a diploma in pastoral theology in year four.

With an average of twelve students in each year, there was a student body of nearly fifty in the college when I was there. Also, another ten post-graduate students lodged at the Beda attending other universities.

The seminarians came from all over the world.

In my year, there were two other Irishmen from the Ferns and Limerick dioceses. Also, we had three other classmates whose parents were Irish and four other Irish students scattered in the other years.

The Beda's students ranged in age from thirty to seventy and came from all kinds of backgrounds. We had ex-bankers, plumbers, postmen and even Christian Brothers among our numbers.

My whole journey to the Beda began in thanksgiving for all the consolations and assurances that I received.

I told Jesus that I would do whatever he asked of me. If that had been digging ditches or delivering meals on wheels, I'd gladly have done that. I was expecting it to be something along those lines.

It still felt surreal to be on a path to priesthood. I arrived full of doubts, but I soon discovered the atmosphere was relaxed and casual.

We were all mature men, so there were no strict rules, regulations or curfews.

The accommodation was simple and basic. We all had a small single room with washbasins, and there were shared shower and toilet block facilities on each floor. A washing machine, dryer and ironing board were also available on each floor.

We had a small kitchen staff and a few cleaning and maintenance staff whose numbers were complemented by the seminarians.

The common areas were something like you'd find in senior common rooms at college. We had a bar, pool table and television room which the seminarians managed.

Outside there was an all-weather soccer pitch, a tennis court and a small gym.

The dress code was student style too with open-neck shirts and casual pants rather than clerical collars, except on Sundays. Clerical clothing was required for mass and Sunday lunch.

I discovered that the day started at 7.00am with mass and prayers in the chapel, followed by lectures until lunch. Most afternoons were free or for completing projects and essays. Evening prayers were at 7.00pm followed by supper.

Evenings were our own and many wiled away the hours before bed in the college bar or watching TV. We also had access to a swimming pool next door.

The Beda is located in Ostiense which was once a working-class area of the city but is now very hip, full of students and street art.

With the metro nearby, all the museums, buildings, art galleries and beautiful parks of the Eternal City were also on our doorstep.

The diocese paid for full board and lectures. Students only had to fund their textbooks and all other living expenses.

Overall, the Beda was a relaxed and serene place.

I soon started feeling comfortable and confident again. It was a long way from home, but it felt like the right place for me to begin my studies for the priesthood.

All the hurdles that seemed so great in the beginning seemed to melt away.

I was relieved to discover during orientation that we could expect a four or five-day break on average about every five weeks.

With breaks for Christmas, Saint Patrick's Day, Easter, summer holidays, and mid-semester breaks, there were many opportunities to go home.

There were two flights per day between Rome to Dublin, and once I booked in advance, they cost less than €100 return. It meant that I didn't have to leave it too long to get back to visit Liz and the children.

I didn't find the academic side of things too difficult either.

I'd read so many books on science, philosophy and religion that I'd already covered a lot of what we were studying.

And I found theology and philosophy far more interesting than the engineering and management subjects I'd studied in my youth.

All I wanted to read about or discuss was theology and philosophy.

I still love learning anything that provides an insight into where Liz, our children and the rest of our loved ones are. So, the study was not the chore I expected it to be.

Also, it turned out that living in a close community, was just what I needed at that point in my life. I was never alone, and I discovered it was a blessing rather than a burden.

All this had become apparent to me by the time we broke for our first Christmas break in 2010. I was a different man by the time I boarded the plane to return home.

All I could say was: *"Thank you, Jesus. I should have known that you knew best all along. Please let Liz's intercessions through your Blessed Mother continue. With their help, I am pretty sure I can make it."*

The only real problem I experienced in the early days at the Beda was not being able to talk about Liz.

When I was among my family and friends, I spoke about Liz every day. When I got to Rome, it was hard to adjust to rarely mentioning her. It wasn't that anyone told me that I couldn't talk about Liz.

But we'd all shared our life journey when we first arrived. People told their stories, and everyone had their concerns.

Some had given up great careers; others were selling homes to fund their day-to-day expenses. Some felt guilty for leaving ageing or sick parents behind.

So, having shared my story, it didn't feel appropriate to raise it every day.

Yet all these memories of Liz and the consolations of faith I'd received buzzed around in my head.

On arriving home for Christmas that first year, I received an avalanche of cards and messages wishing me well. Everyone remarked what a special person Liz was.

These people lived all around Ireland and some as far afield as America. I would not get the opportunity to meet some of them for many years.

Touched by all the beautiful messages, I vowed when I returned to the Beda, that I'd write an account of the amazing consolations I'd received through Liz.

I promised to send them on to all these people who took the time to express their love and admiration for Liz.

Writing these turned out to be another great blessing in the New Year. As I started to write, it was like reliving all the wonderful experiences I had.

As we had to cram six years of work into four, we had a lot of projects and essays to complete.

I concentrated on working on the assignments all week so that I had the luxury of using my weekends to write up my account of the consolations.

I found it a great release, very therapeutic and a good way to cope with my grief.

The rector of the Beda, Monsignor Roderick Strange, made it his job to appoint seminarians to their house positions.

The second-year class of seminarians usually take on the bigger jobs while the men in the rest of the years become their foot soldiers.

Some jobs came with a lot of responsibility and were time-consuming positions.

The head of the refectory who looked after the dining room had a difficult job, and so did the bar manager in the Beda.

The master of ceremonies, who was responsible for the smooth running of all the masses and observances, had a busy schedule.

And whoever was sacristan had to look after the sacristy, sacred vessels, and vestments and had significant duties in the church too.

All these appointments were at Monsignor Strange's discretion, and we knew that they weren't up for negotiation or discussion.

I worked as a foot soldier in year one in the sacristy doing background preparation for all of the liturgies.

I'd learnt over many years in management how to pace myself. I knew how to conserve physical, mental, emotional and spiritual energies for a campaign.

Emotionally, I was still recovering from grief, and mentally I was still adjusting to getting back to full-time studies in my sixties.

I wanted to focus on doing everything I could to complete my four years of studies and priestly formation.

I felt the stress and the time demands of one of the more difficult jobs could put my primary objective at risk.

I was apprehensive about approaching the rector, but at the end of year one, I felt I had to. My success in the Beda depended on it.

I explained to the rector that I didn't mind cleaning, scrubbing, digging or taking orders. But I requested, if at all possible, that he wouldn't appoint me to any of the responsible positions in the Beda.

Monsignor Strange was a genial and thoughtful man as I discovered. He didn't get annoyed by me approaching him in this way.

He said he appreciated my honesty and courage and also appreciated that I had the wisdom to know my limitations. He said he'd take my request into consideration.

As we wound up the meeting, he asked: *"What type of role do you feel would best suit you, Sean?"*

I immediately said I'd love to work in the garden.

When he announced the house jobs in September, my position was in the garden. And he appointed me to the garden each year after that.

Given my background in farming and working on the land, it was the perfect job for me.

It was a pleasure after a morning of lectures to spend an hour or two working in the Beda's garden.

I thank God every day for Monsignor Strange's understanding and support.

I didn't have any more explicit experiences or consolations during my time in the Beda, but I accepted this.

I understood they were for a particular time and purpose. And they had culminated in me being at the Beda studying for the priesthood.

Still, I had one lovely experience thanks to the kindness of a classmate.

In the third year, we practised composing and delivering short homilies.

The lecturer recorded us as we presented our writings to our classmates. Afterwards, he played back the videos and critiqued us on content and delivery.

The Beda fosters a caring and supportive system between the students, so it was never too much of an ordeal. But still, there was a certain amount of anxiety before any of these class presentations.

One night, I put the finishing touches to a sermon that I was due to deliver the next morning. But I had picked up a cold earlier, and that night it morphed into a chest infection.

As soon as I went to bed, it became a hacking cough; it was impossible to sleep. I didn't have a cough bottle or lozenge or anything that would relieve it.

I recall complaining to Jesus: *"Here I am, trying to do my best. I want the delivery of my homily to go well in the morning. This is a great time to develop a cough. I'll get no sleep, and then I'll be coughing and spluttering during my delivery."*

The floors in the hallways and rooms of the Beda are tiled, so every noise echoed through the place. I was conscious of everyone else on the floor trying to sleep, so I did my best to keep the hacking down.

But around 3.00am, I heard a knock on the door. I hoped it wasn't someone coming to complain that my coughing was keeping them awake.

The late night caller was my classmate from two rooms down, Patrick Daly, from England.

Patrick knew all about Liz, and I'd shared some of the consolations I'd had with him.

He said he'd woken up, heard my coughing, and then he turned over to go back to sleep again. Then he said he kept hearing the words in his head: *"Liz, Liz, Liz....Liz, Liz, Liz..."*

He said to himself: *"Liz will never forgive me if I don't get up and help Sean."*

So, he handed me a hot drink with lemon in it, and he went back to bed.

Even though Patrick couldn't have known, the chant "Liz, Liz, Liz" had another meaning for me.

As a youth, I played Gaelic football, but after living in Canada and America, I'd fallen out of touch with the sport.

Then in 2003, our home county Laois came good, and Liz, through her family, knew a rising star on the team called Ross Munnelly.

There was great excitement as the Laois stormed through the Leinster quarter-finals, semi-final and then to the final.

We went along to the games with the Munnellys and Liz's family. Liz bought a lovely straw hat with the Laois colours which I still keep.

The chant that year was *"Laois, Laois, Laois"* said in rapid succession. Liz was an expert when it came to chanting it.

When Patrick told his story, and he described hearing *"Liz, Liz, Liz"* in quick succession, his English accent made it sound like *"Laois, Laois, Laois."*

It was the first time I'd heard that in years.

I thanked him, had my hot drink and went off to sleep.

I hadn't the slightest doubt that Liz had urged him to come to my aid.

Not only that, but she'd given him a little code which let me know, without a doubt, that this hot drink was from Liz.

We were ordained as Deacons at end of year three in the historical Saint Paul's Cathedral across the road from the Beda.

One of Rome's four major Papal basilicas, the Cathedral, provides a very grand and stately resting place for Saint Paul.

And the ceremony was as solemn and dignified as our imposing surroundings.

My family and Liz's sister, Margaret, flew to Rome to attend as did Bishop Jim Moriarty and my diocesan vocations director, Father Ruairi O'Domhnaill.

Saint Paul's soaring acoustics also provided the perfect stage for our rector, Monsignor Strange, who is a polished orator.

After the ordination ceremony, he congratulated the nine candidates in our year. He welcomed all the families, priests and Bishops who had travelled to Rome for the occasion.

He mentioned family members and friends who could not travel due to illness or infirmity and remembered deceased parents and friends of the candidates.

Winding up, he said: "We especially remember Sean's family, his children and his beloved wife, Liz."

Then with his impeccable timing, he paused and let the Basilica's magical acoustics do the rest of his work.

I heard Liz's name echo around that awe-inspiring cathedral and hang in the air for a beautiful moment.

Monsignor Strange had a sense of drama and grandeur and knew how to stage formal occasions in style.

The college had a fine dining room along with beautiful silverware, tableware bearing the Beda crest and sparkling crystal glassware.

All was laid out in full palatial pomp for formal occasions in the Beda.

The kitchen staff, while small in number, included a top-class chef who served only the best of food and finest wines.

During the four years to the priesthood, there were many important milestones along the way for the students.

Monsignor Strange organised it so that we celebrated one such occasion every six weeks or so.

We had Cardinals and Archbishops attending all grand, formal dinner occasions.

But the social highlight of the year was the lunch hosted after the Deacons' ordination ceremony.

All the men from the other years did the serving and support for the day.

Meanwhile, we, the newly ordained deacons, sat among hundreds of visiting family and friends and basked in the glory of the big day.

The buffet lunch, which had all the grandeur of royal banquet, was hosted in the beautiful gardens.

And I like to think that my gardening contributed more than a little to the enjoyment and splendour of the day.

A Reflection on Learning in the Beda

One lecturer, an American Redemptorist priest, stands out in my memories of the Beda.

He was our professor of moral theology, and he was renowned at all the universities in Rome. He was considered world class in particular for his lectures on the Seven Virtues.

Virtues are defined as 'habitual and firm dispositions to do good', and the most well-known ones are faith, hope and charity.

This priest was passionate about the Seven Virtues. He would plead with us as mature seminarians, never to just philosophise or preach about them.

He tried very hard to ensure we understood that we had to live the Virtues. They had to become a way of life for a priest. He'd say how preaching without living them is hypocritical and worse than a waste of time.

We had to live the Virtues and teach by example rather than lecturing about them.

Hope, faith and charity are known as the Moral Virtues. Then there are the four Cardinal Virtues which are fortitude, justice, prudence and temperance.

Faith means we believe in God; hope means we trust that we merit eternal life, and charity means we love our neighbour as ourselves.

And charity is the big one as it 'binds everything in perfect harmony'.

Saint Paul's 'Theological Virtues' of Love, hope and faith is a slight variation on these.

Paul insisted that love was the highest virtue of all. But many argue that charity and love overlap, and any difference is due to the translation from ancient texts.

I will always remember that priest pleading with us to understand and internalise the Virtues and to live by them.

By following the Virtues, he exhorted, we would be seen to be virtuous people, and others were more likely to follow our example.

I wanted to shout out that I knew exactly what he meant because I lived with someone who lived the Virtues and by her example, she saved me.

I watched Liz, for over forty-two years, not just grow into the Virtues but to radiate them in everything she did and said.

I can vouch for the impact this kind of goodness can have even on the slowest of learners. It was her goodness and example that turned me around and changed my life.

The Beda also taught us to live according to the eight beatitudes of Christ. The Beatitudes are a list of all things held to be good in the eyes of Jesus.

Jesus says:
"Blessed are the poor in spirit, for theirs is the kingdom of heaven.
Blessed are they who mourn, for they shall be comforted.
Blessed are the meek, for they shall inherit the earth.
Blessed are they who hunger and thirst for righteousness,
for they shall be satisfied.
Blessed are the merciful, for they shall obtain mercy.
Blessed are the pure of heart, for they shall see God.
Blessed are the peacemakers, for they shall be called children of God.
Blessed are they who are persecuted for the sake of righteousness,
for theirs is the kingdom of heaven."
Gospel of St. Matthew 5:3-10

I've often thought that combining the Seven Virtues with the Beatitudes, gives us a simple handbook on how to become a saint.

By simple, I mean it's easy to understand what we need to do. We don't need a degree in theology or need great mystical experiences to know what we need to do.

What's not so simple is following this simple handbook. But then, if it was easy to follow, there would be a lot more saints around.

Saints are people who live the Virtues and follow the Beatitudes through good times and bad, through joy, pain, fear and grief.

Liz would never have claimed to be a saint, but she managed to live the Virtues.

And we all know people who live their lives closely to these guidelines.

These are special people, who are well advanced on the path of a virtuous life.

It's not only a blessing to be in the company of people like this, but a great joy. They can make goodness appear effortless.

I often say to people I will never be a Padre Pio, a John Paul II or a Mother Teresa. But I can be more like Liz or like my father. That's all I need to be.

As I said, I'm a slow learner, and I don't always succeed in living the Virtues.

But I don't give up. I continually pray to the Virgin Mary and her Son to grant me the grace to live the Virtues.

12

The Apprentice

"And Christ called to him the twelve,
and began to send them out two by two,
and gave them authority over unclean spirits...
So, they went out and preached that men should repent.
And they cast out many demons and anointed with oil
many that were sick and healed them."
Mark 6: 7, 12-13

As part of our assignments in the Beda, seminarians completed a six-week pastoral placement in their diocese every summer.

Placement entailed moving in with a priest and assisting him with all his daily duties. We also had to keep a log of all our activities and to make note of any spiritual insights we had.

Then we were expected to write a report of our placement when we returned to the Beda.

My very first placement took place in Carbury parish, a small rural town in Kildare, less than an hour from home in Portarlington.

I stayed with the parish priest, Father John Fitzpatrick, for the duration of the placement. I served at mass each morning, visited the sick of the parish and sat in on school and parish committee meetings.

He kept a small room in the parochial house with the Blessed Sacrament displayed in a small monstrance for adoration.

During the day, he liked to use the room as a place of prayer, while I went to the chapel for prayers and contemplation.

Father John was a marathon runner who went for long runs in the evenings.

While he was out running, I spent long periods in that room with the Blessed Sacrament and with his library of books.

Early on in the placement, I picked out a book called 'The End Times as Revealed to Maria Valtorta.'

Maria was an Italian writer, devoted Catholic and mystic who claimed to talk to Jesus.

She recorded in writing all the words of Jesus and many of his detailed descriptions of his time on earth.

In the 20 years before her death in 1961, she penned over 15,000 handwritten pages in 122 notebooks.

In the book, The End Times, Maria recounts a series of visions she had of Jesus decoding the Book of Revelations.

I felt privileged to sit for long periods in front of the Blessed Sacrament reading the words of Jesus decoding the Book of Revelations.

When I mentioned this to Father John, he pointed out that he had four volumes of 'The Poem of the Man-God' by Maria Valtorta on his bookshelves.

Spending nights in front of the Blessed Sacrament reading extracts from these volumes became part of a cherished routine.

I happened to start with volume three, at a part that describes Jesus trying to reconcile profound differences between Anne of Kerioth and Mary of Simon.

Valtorta's writings explain that Mary of Simon is the mother of Judas Iscariot. The two women are not talking because Judas has abruptly and cruelly broken off his engagement to the daughter of Anne of Kerioth.

Jesus also knows that Mary will soon be heartbroken by her son's betrayal, her son's death by suicide and by His death on the cross.

So, he wants to ensure that the two women reunite before Mary's losses.

Reading this account, I was struck by the incredible love and care that Jesus exhibits in his efforts to reconcile the warring women.

He cares about the women's problems at such a personal and human level that it reminded me of my own experiences.

The consolations of faith I received in the year after Liz's death let me feel the powerful presence of God in my life. The fact that the Creator of this world would come to console me was almost overwhelming.

Reading Maria Valtorta's books reminded me that Jesus loves, supports and consoles us on a personal level when we call out in faith.

I still value that placement in Carberry and hold fond memories of evenings in front of the Blessed Sacrament reading the words of Jesus.

My second-year Pastoral Placement took place in Carlow town which is about 45 minutes away from my home.

Carlow is the Cathedral parish for our Diocese of Kildare and Leighlin which covers 56 parishes across seven counties.

My placement with Father John Cummins was another great privilege and learning experience.

Despite running a busy parish, it was clear that Father John is a deeply reflective and prayerful priest. I was glad to see at close quarters how important this is in the life of a priest even in a demanding post.

He gave me a wide range of tasks which made me feel like I was making a valuable contribution to the life of the parish.

We worked closely with the clerics of three other churches, so teamwork was an essential part of the placement.

According to canon law only ordained priests can deliver a homily. I did the next best thing for practical experience - which is to deliver a brief reflection after communion.

For the first time, I led the prayers at funerals and at communion which gave me a real sense of pastoral ministry.

Also, for the first time, I felt the serious responsibility of communicating the presence of God to people, particularly in their hour of need.

One of my jobs was to assist Sister Dolores who led the prayers and distributed communion in St. Dymnpa's psychiatric hospital in Carlow.

Many of the patients had a limited attention span and were difficult to engage in conversation.

But I watched Sister Dolores' gentle and casual interactions. She greeted each patient, and if they didn't respond after a couple of efforts, she moved on to the next person.

But I noticed how she always kept coming back to the person who didn't respond again and again. She kept going until she succeeded in making a connection and getting a response of a smile or a handshake.

After the second week, the Sister went on leave, so it was up to me to distribute communion on my own. Taking the Sister's cue, I stayed on after the communion to engage in conversation with the patients.

I tried to copy Sister Dolores' relaxed and easy approach but with limited success. I'm not a natural carer or socialiser, and I'm sure the patients could see that I was a bit uncomfortable and ill at ease.

I was a little frustrated and disappointed that I wasn't able to step into Sister Dolores' shoes.

As the weeks progressed, my success rate improved and some of the patients responded to me. But despite my efforts, I still failed to connect with many of the patients.

Father John and Sister Dolores were very kind and insisted my expectations were too high. The Sister said she had a lot of experience in working with psychiatric patients and was very familiar with this set of patients.

Despite their reassurances, I left this placement knowing that I needed a lot more experience and work on this area of pastoral ministry.

Since then, I've tried to develop the great gift Liz had for living in the present.

Whatever we did together, Liz was always fully engaged in it. If we went to an art gallery, Liz would want to stop and appreciate every picture.

I wanted to see the important paintings, and then I'd get restless and want to move on and go somewhere else.

Liz was the same when it came to dealing with people. She wanted to talk and get to know them, while I got bored with conversation and wanted to move on to the next thing.

I always wanted '*to do*' rather than '*be*'.

I understand the value of living in the present now. It allows you to connect with people and show them the respect that they're due.

It allows you to appreciate everything and everyone around you.

Summer placements showed me the enormous responsibility and privilege that comes with the pastoral role. They also highlighted my short-comings.

Because I need as much inspiration and guidance as I can get in the role of a priest, I hold one Biblical quote close to my heart.

It was the opening sentence of a reading given to me by my vocations' director in 2009

The full quote from Jeremiah 3:15 reads: *"I will give you shepherds after my own heart. They will be shepherds who feed you with knowledge and insight."*

I'm not a priest formed like God's own heart yet, and I can't say that I'm full of knowledge and insight, but at least I'm striving towards the goal.

The second piece of inspiration I like to read is a poem I first saw printed on the back of an ordination card. It's like a mandate for a priest.

Written by nineteenth-century French priest and journalist, Jean-Baptiste Henri Lacordaire, this poem inspires me every time.

You can hear and feel his passion for his role as a priest when he exclaims: *"My God, what a life!"*

That's the way I started to feel after my first couple of years in the Beda and after my first placements. My confidence began to grow. I could discern a message that told me: *"Yes, this is how it can be, and you're on track so far."*

The sense of privilege and responsibility was tremendous, and so was my sense of awe about my new life as a priest.

Thou Art a Priest Forever
To live in the midst of the world without
desiring its pleasures;
To be a member of each family
yet belonging to none;
To share all sufferings;
To penetrate all secrets;
To heal all wounds;
To go from men to God and offer Him their prayers;
To return from God to men to bring pardon, peace and hope;
To have a heart of fire for charity and a heart of bronze for chastity;
To teach and to pardon, to console and to bless always;
My God, what a life!
And it is yours, O Priest of Jesus Christ!

13

Consolations Through Seana

"Let the little children come to me, and do not hinder them,
for the kingdom of heaven belongs to such as these."
Matthew 19:14

Our daughter Seana was born on Monday, April 16, 1973, and I know every father adores his little girl, but she was a special child.

She was very advanced for her age. She wasn't even two-years-old when she died, but she was precocious; more like a three-year-old.

For the first year of her life, she stayed in a cot in our bedroom. Then Liz made plans to move Seana to her own bedroom.

She did it with fanfare and celebrations so that Seana would feel grown-up and independent rather than ousted. Seana loved to feel grown-up.

The two of them went to Mountmellick, and together they bought a little white wardrobe and dressing table for Seana's new room.

There was great excitement when the delivery men arrived, and they placed the new furniture in the bedroom along with Seana's cot.

As soon as I came in the door from work that evening, Seana ran to me, grabbed me by the hand and dragged me down the hall to her new room.

"Seana's lobdrobe!" she squealed with delight. *"Look! Seana's lobdrobe!"*

I can see her still running from the wardrobe at one wall, to the dressing table on the other and back again as she showed me her new things; her own room; her own space.

She was so excited. *"Look, Daddy, Seana's lobdrobe!"*

She couldn't quite get her tongue around the word 'wardrobe', but we daren't laugh at her pronunciation. Seana prided herself on being very capable.

It was vital to keep a straight face when she extolled the virtues of her new 'lobdrobe', or she'd go mad altogether.

Do all little girls like watches? I don't know, but Seana wanted a watch from the time she was tiny.

We bought her one when she was 18-months-old. She wanted it, and she got it. Any photographs that were taken after that, I can see her wearing that watch.

My Sunday morning job was to get Seana ready for mass. I'd comb her hair while making sure to admire 'Seana's lovely hair.'

Her hair was light and a bit wispy, but she loved it being brushed, and she loved hearing about *'Seana's lovely hair'*.

I wasn't the most conscientious about mass or God at that time, so I didn't see the harm in being five minutes late. We all went to 'the crying room' anyway.

This family room, right up near the altar, was the place where parents could bring young children. Surrounded by soundproof glass, it allowed other mass-goers to have peace and quiet from the distractions of kids.

Liz never liked us leaving late and always watched the clock.

And as soon as Liz pointed meaningfully at her watch and tapped it with her index finger, that would be it. She wouldn't say anything, but it was clear that my time for dossing around had run out.

Seana picked up her mother's habit remarkably fast.

She was the spitting image of me when I was a child even down to the little dimple she had. But personality wise, she was a little Liz.

If she thought it was time for her tea, for example, she'd look at me severely, point to her watch and tap it exactly like her mother.

"*Seana's tea!*" she'd instruct.

When I say she was a little Liz, I mean that.

Liz was impeccable; she was a complete perfectionist around the house. I wasn't a slob; I'd be tidy, but I wasn't fanatical about cleaning.

But after a few years of living with a perfectionist, you pick up the same habits, and you live up to the same standards.

It wasn't that Liz imposed her perfectionism on me, but I knew that it upset her when things weren't neat and ordered.

If there was a fleck of white fluff or anything on the carpet, Liz couldn't pass it by. She'd have to pick it up.

Seana was exactly the same. She'd spot a speck on the carpet at fifty paces and would run to pick it up.

If there wasn't a bin handy, she'd present it to me and expect it to be disposed of straight away. Seana didn't have to be told. She knew that's what you do.

What flowed between Liz and Seana was incredible. It was like only their years separated them. She was like Liz's little clone.

Liz met up often with her friend Dolores who had a girl, Eileen, the same age as Seana, and a baby boy, Thomas.

Eileen and Seana played together all the time.

Dolores told me about a day when she and Liz treated the kids to ice creams.

Dolores handed the ices to Thomas and Eileen who soon had cream all over their faces and hands.

Liz, being a perfectionist, tried to hold the ice cream for Seana.

Seana, who wasn't even two, refused to stand for this babyish treatment.

"*Thomas icecream… Seana icecream!*" she glowered.

She was so small, but her logic was clear: "If even the baby can hold his own ice cream, so can I!"

Seana was never sick a day in her life. She was full of energy, a picture of health and had all her vaccinations.

The week before Saint Patrick's day in March 1975, Seana already had her first Saint Patrick's badge.

She could hardly wait to wear it, and she showed it to me every evening when I came in the door.

But I got home on Thursday, March 10, Liz was making the dinner, and there was no sign of Seana.

She had a case of the sniffles earlier on, but now Liz said she had a bit of a temperature.

"*I think you should go up and get the doctor*," she said.

We built our house down a lane off the main road in Portarlington, but back in 1975, we had no phone. It took years to get a phone then.

I went down to see Seana, and she was coughing a little, but she was sleeping, and it didn't seem that serious.

Still, I told Liz that I wouldn't wait for the dinner. I went straight down to the dispensary where our family medic, Doctor Laurence Fullam, worked.

He got his coat and came up with me in the car straight away, and when we got to the house, Seana was dead.

They told us afterwards that she had contracted a virulent viral pneumonia which overwhelmed her.

Seana would have been two-years-old the following month.

Fast forward with me to Tuesday, September 24, 2013.

It was the final day of my summer holidays in Ireland, and I was flying back to Rome the next morning to begin my fourth and last year in the Beda.

Over the years, I had settled into a routine of travelling home from the Beda to Ireland during each break in the semester every five weeks or so.

That way the Beda became a series of short sprints of five or six weeks each rather than a marathon of four years.

At this stage, I'd also been ordained a Deacon in Saint Paul's Cathedral in Rome, and most of the heavy lifting in studies was behind me.

I also had the luxury of spending my third summer placement in my own hometown of Portarlington with Father Tom Dooley. By now I had a good understanding of the role of a priest in a parish in Ireland, and I was enjoying the role.

Even without any explicit consolations of faith, I experienced a great peace of mind during this time. I had a lot to be thankful for.

That afternoon, following my usual routine, I went to Saint Michael's church in Portarlington to say the Divine Mercy Chaplet.

I was kneeling before the altar in the deserted church when I heard footsteps coming up the aisle.

A woman with a little girl aged about two passed me to light a candle right in front of the altar.

The child hauled herself up onto the seat in front of me. Her head was almost at my left shoulder because I was kneeling.

Liz's memorial card was on the seat in front of me where I could gaze at it as I prayed.

The card has the image of Our Lord of Divine Mercy on the front and a photo of Liz, Seana and Kieran inside it.

The little girl picked up the memory card. I didn't mind because I had more cards even if she ran away with it.

I pointed to the photos and said: "*That's Liz and Seana and Kieran.*"

She understood that these people were important to me because she placed the card back on the seat carefully.

"*My name's Sean,*" I said. "*What's yours?*"

"*Elisa,*" she said.

I could have spent hours talking to her, but I saw her mother look over her shoulder.

It dawned on me that she might worry about a sixty-year-old stranger talking to her little girl, so I returned to my prayers.

As two-year-olds do, Elisa ran off, and then she ran back, and then she pulled herself up on the seat again and squirmed around so she could face me for a chat.

She chattered all about her dad. It sounded like he might be on shift work, and they had just dropped him off.

Conscious of the mother keeping a watchful eye, I didn't encourage the conversation, and the little girl went back to her mother.

Then the woman and Elisa approached me, and the mother asked if there was a toilet in the church.

I indicated the door behind the family room but added that it was probably locked during the day.

They went over, but then they went out the side door nearby, so it was clear the toilet was locked.

I finished my prayers and was at the main exit when the woman and Elisa reappeared in front of me.

The woman looked a bit unsure, but she said: "*Don't ask me to explain this, because Elisa doesn't give hugs and certainly not to strange men.*

"*But as soon as I started the car, she begged me to let her come back into the church. She says she wants to give you a big hug.*"

I looked down at Elisa who looked back at me with a wide-eyed and solemn expression.

Her face told me she had offered me something special, and she hoped that I understood and accepted it.

My mind started to race; I wanted to get my part in this important ceremony right.

I knew exactly what a big deal it was for her to give a hug because my Seana was the same.

I remembered how Liz would nearly shudder when effusive American clients pulled her in for a bear hug at the end of business dinners.

She always smiled gamely, but I knew never liked it.

Seana was like her mother in this. Back in the 70s, everyone thought it was okay to pick up little girls and hug them.

Seana would return the hug with open arms, but I can still picture her face.

I'd always catch a fleeting glance in her expression that told me these hugs weren't welcome.

No one else would recognise it, but I could read her. That almost imperceptible grimace said: *"Let's just get this over with."*

For Seana, a hug was a gift that she gave to special people. She didn't like it taken from her.

And here I was facing another frugal hugger, and I wanted to let her know that I really appreciated the kind offer.

How does a lumbering sixty-year-old hug a tiny two-year-old?

So many thoughts ran through my head. *I won't pick her up because it might frighten her, or her mother might not like it. If I hunker down, I'm liable to tip over and flatten the child which would be worse.*

A split second later, I thought: *"I'll get down on one knee, that way I'll be at the right height, and I'll be stable."*

I desperately wanted to get this right for Elisa.

As I got down to receive a big hug from this little girl, it seemed like a luminous image appeared in my mind's eye. I could see large golden gates way off the distance. The gates were wide open, with no one at them.

It was then I realised I was seeing the gates of heaven, and that I was receiving a precious gift from heaven from Seana through Elisa.

I barely managed to stumble to my feet afterwards. I wanted to take Liz's memorial card from my pocket and explain to the mother, the great gift Elisa had given me.

But I was struck dumb with emotion; I couldn't say a word.

As articulation was impossible, I bowed with both hands joined together in thanks instead.

The mother may have been a little disappointed that I wasn't more effusive in my praise for Elisa.

But she must have seen the tears brimming in my eyes and realised there was more going on than she or I understood.

I watched as they walked towards their car.

The last thing I saw was Elisa giving a little skip, the way two-year-olds do when they're happy, or they know they've done something good.

I never got the registration number of the car or any contact details. I would have loved to invite Elisa and her mother to my ordination the following year.

I've never forgotten that day. How could I?

It was my little Seana reaching out to me again. This consolation through Seana came at a time when I felt at peace.

I hadn't any urgent needs. Yet out of the blue, I received this great gift. And I hope if that mother ever hears this story, she'll call me so I can thank Elisa properly for bringing that gift to me.

A Reflection on the Loss of a Child in Verse

After Seana's death, someone gave me a copy of the following famous poem by the late American poet, Edgar Albert Guest.

It's a poem that has been bringing comfort to grief-stricken parents for decades.

He suffered the loss of two of his children too, and he thought that focusing on the gift of the time he had with his children brought a measure of comfort.

Edgar Guest was right. I often read this, and always find some consolation in his lovely words.

A Child of Mine

"I'll lend you for a while a child of mine," He said.
"For you to love the while he lives and mourn for when he's dead.
It may be six or seven years, or twenty-two or three,
But will you, till I call him back, take care of him for me?
He'll bring his charms to gladden you, and should his stay be brief,
You'll have his lovely memories as solace for your grief."

"I cannot promise he will stay; since all from earth return,
But there are lessons taught down there I want this child to learn.
I've looked the wide world over in My search for teachers true
And from the throngs that crowd life's lanes, I have chosen you.
Now will you give him all your love, not think the labour vain,
Nor hate Me when I come to call to take him back again?"

"I fancied that I heard them say, "Dear Lord, Thy will be done!
For all the joy Thy child shall bring, the risk of grief we run.

We'll shelter him with tenderness, we'll love him while we may,
And for the happiness we've known, forever grateful stay;
But should the angels call for him much sooner than we've planned,
We'll brave the bitter grief that comes and try to understand!"

A Reflection on Grief and Suffering

In the Old Testament, we read about Job's endless sufferings after a series of disasters.

He has lost his offspring, his fortune and his health. Poor Job is afflicted with sores, from the soles of his feet to the crown of his head. The only thing Job has not lost is his faith in God.

Why should a good and innocent man face such a fate? Job's friends suggest that he must have sinned and urge him to admit his guilt before God.

Job protests that he hasn't sinned and he has always loved God and his neighbour.

Job knows that his suffering is not a consequence of sin, but he has no answer to the eternal question of the persecuted: "Why me?"

Job perseveres, doesn't question his afflictions or moan about injustice.

Then God shows mercy and Job's sufferings end, and he regains even greater health, wealth and more offspring.

It's hard not to rail against injustice and wonder why innocent people suffer.

Even Jesus has his own *'Why me?"* moment on the cross when he cries out:

"My God, my God, why have you forsaken me?" Matthew 27:46

It shows His real humanity, and how much He is suffering to say this.

Because Jesus makes it clear in the gospels that everyone will bear their own crosses whether they are believers or not.

He tells us the sun shines and the rain falls on the good and the evil alike.

Instead of crying *'Why me?'*, Jesus urges us to carry our crosses.

He said to his disciples: *"If anyone would come after me, let him deny himself and take up his cross and follow me."* Matthew 16:24

He doesn't ask us to go looking for crosses. Nor does he say that if we become a true disciple, we will encounter extra or more difficult crosses.

But if we humbly accept the request to take up our cross and follow Him, we will discover the cross is not as fearful as it appears at first glance.

Also, Jesus asks us to ease the burden of other people's crosses.

Anytime Jesus is confronted with the sufferings of other people, he never dwells on *'why?'*

He never asks if they deserve this infliction and never judges the ill and the desperate.

He just moves to heal all human suffering and cure the afflicted.

Once the word is out about Jesus, every sick and suffering person in the region descends on him. And Jesus has an emergency ward on his hands.

We can see God's care in the commitment of doctors, nurses, healers, hospital chaplains and all the people who tend to the suffering of others. They are God's compassion in the flesh, God's care in motion.

No doubt all have reason to wonder, to protest, to be angry when they see the innocent suffer. But they carry on. That is their enduring witness. Like Jesus, they know that the schedule of care must be kept.

The iconic image for every Christian is the suffering, crucified Christ. Jesus suffered, and he expected to suffer.

And the good and the innocent will suffer and do suffer.

The Apostle Peter says: *"Rejoice insofar as you share Christ's sufferings, that you may also rejoice and be glad at his glory."* 1 Peter 4:12.

If we take up our crosses and follow Jesus, suffering can be positive, prayerful and sacrificial.

We know that Jesus cares; that he shares our suffering and Jesus can transform our pain.

Ask, and you shall receive. I know from my own experience that Jesus always ensures we receive the grace we need to bear our suffering and to carry our crosses.

Jesus suffered, and it was His path to glory.

And that's the whole point.

Suffering, grief and loss is a part of life, but it can also be if we let it, part of our path to glory.

14

The Mystical Rose

"The flowers appear on the earth, the time of singing has come,
and the voice of the turtledove is heard in our land."

Song of Solomon 2:12

When I came home for Christmas in my final year of the Beda, I learnt the Bishop had set the date for my ordination for Sunday, July 13, 2014.

Once I got back to Rome, I Skyped a fellow student, who was still in Lithuania and told him of my ordination date.

"July 13 is the feast of The Mystical Rose!" he said immediately.

"What's that?" I asked.

"I don't know," he admitted. *"I just know that July 13 is the feast day of the Mystical Rose."*

I asked my fellow seminarians, who were much better versed in feast days than I was, but they were puzzled too.

"Sorry, never heard of it," was the most common response.

Knowing my Lithuanian friend was rarely wrong about anything, I searched on the internet for 'the feast of the Mystical Rose.'

There I discovered that Our Blessed Lady revealed herself as Mary the Mystical Rose to a humble Italian visionary in 1947 - the year of my birth.

Nurse Pierina Gilli was in the hospital chapel in Montichiari, Italy when she received the first apparition of the Virgin Mary.

Mary appeared to her in dazzling light and wearing three roses: one white, one red and one golden yellow.

The white rose symbolises the spirit of prayer; the red rose represents the spirit of sacrifice, and the yellow rose is for the spirit of penance.

During another apparition on July 13, Our Lady asked for prayer, sacrifice and penance from priests.

She also asked for July 13 to be celebrated in honour of the Rosa Mystica every year.

The apparitions are well known in Italy where the shrine of the Mystical Rose is a popular place of pilgrimage.

Distracted with all of my final year studies, the date for my ordination in Ireland was forgotten about.

I realised there was a lot to organise, but I had no time to deal with it. I was still working on the last of my assignments and studying for final exams in Rome.

The mass would have to be organised like a well-oiled clock. I had to select all the readings and the hymns and produce a commemorative booklet for the Bishop and congregation.

Everything from the flowers to the musicians and singers would also need to be considered.

I had to send out invitations for the ordination and organise a celebratory dinner for everyone.

The problem was, I had no idea how to do any of this. Liz organised every event in my life from parties to business dinners and fundraisers.

And I had no practical training in the Beda. With four fast-paced years of formation, all the focus was on studies of scripture, church history, theology and philosophy.

They told us the practical aspects of being a priest - including organising events - would have to be learnt on the job.

Many of my fellow seminarians had organised the liturgy in their parishes for years. They seemed to find it easy to arrange the mass and produce a special booklet for their ordinations.

I was clueless, and I knew I would be arriving back in Ireland in late June two weeks before the ordination.

Liz always made arranging events look easy, but I didn't even know where to start.

From being someone who had been at peace in my studies, I now felt anxious and stressed.

I knew Our Lady of the Mystical Rose and my ordination day had a special connection. So, if I needed help for my ordination, where better to ask than at the shrine of the Mystical Rose?

I hoped that Liz, through Our Lady, would organise my ordination like she managed everything before for me.

I boarded a train for the four-hour journey from Rome to northern Italy where the shrine of the Mystical Rose is located.

The little town of Montichiari, surrounded by towering mountains, is close to the clear, azure waters of Lake Garda. I stayed overnight in a hotel near the town with plans to take a bus to the shrine the next morning.

That night for the first time in a long time, I had a dream about Liz. I seldom if ever dream about Liz. She's always on my mind, and yet she rarely appears in my sleep. Maybe, it might be too painful to keep seeing her.

In this dream, I understood that Liz was visiting me; she wasn't dead but she had just returned from somewhere after a long time. I was so happy to see her and kept begging her to stay longer.

"*I can't Sean*," she said. "*I have too many things to arrange and organise for you. I haven't time to stay!*"

The next day I visited and prayed at the shrine. I thought about the dream and what Liz had told me. I felt sure that Liz had come to say to me that she was working on all the arrangements for my ordination.

She and Our Lady had everything in hand as usual. I heaved a sigh of relief. I felt it was out of my hands. All I had to do was show up.

And so, it turned out to be.

Our Lady of the Mystical Rose has three coloured roses, but Liz always had a great affinity for yellow or golden roses which stand for the spirit of penance.

Liz's love for golden roses began after Pope John Paul II donated a sprig of roses in gold to Our Lady's shrine in Knock during his 1979 visit to Ireland.

So, for our twentieth wedding anniversary in 1992, I went to a goldsmith and had a gold rose brooch specially designed and manufactured as a surprise for Liz.

For the rest of her life, Liz's three most precious possessions were her engagement ring, her wedding ring and the gold rose brooch.

When we knew Liz was dying, I asked what she'd like me to do with her personal possessions.

She asked me to give her watch to her sister Margaret, her car to her brother Paddy and to ask her sister to divide her clothes and jewellery between all her nieces.

She asked me to keep her engagement ring, her wedding ring and the gold rose brooch.

I did what Liz requested except I didn't give away her jewellery. Everything in her jewellery box came with memories that I couldn't part with.

I gave the jewellery to my brother for safe keeping when I went to Rome apart from her wedding and engagement rings which I took with me.

On the train journey home from the visit to the Mystical Rose shrine, I suddenly thought with a shock that I hadn't seen Liz's gold rose brooch in a long time.

I tried to remember where I'd last seen it. I had Liz's engagement and wedding rings in a purse with me in Rome which I kept by my bedside. I always assumed that the rose brooch was with them, but now I wasn't sure.

I rushed back to the Beda to see if the rose was there. My heart sank when I looked in the purse, and there was no sign of Liz's rose.

I phoned P.J.

"Can you check Liz's jewellery and see if her golden rose brooch is in there?" I asked.

He rummaged in the jewellery box and came back to the phone.

"No sign of it, Sean. It's not with everything else."

"Would you have a look in my house to see if you can find it? I don't understand where it can have got to."

The next day P.J. said he couldn't find it in the house either.

I racked my brain for days trying to figure out where it might be. I couldn't think of any other place I'd put it.

The rose was so precious to Liz, and I felt it had even more significance now with the Mystical Rose connection. I couldn't wait to get home to Portarlington to search the house again.

While I was in Rome, I rented the house in Rathvilly where Liz and I lived before she died. I had cleared it out completely before the tenants moved in, so I knew it wasn't there.

Liz's missing golden rose weighed heavily on my mind. The thought of losing it upset me a lot.

I returned to Ireland shortly afterwards for Saint Patrick's Day on March 17.

Coming home must have jogged my memory, and I recalled last seeing the gold rose on the lapel of one of Liz's favourite jackets.

It's a classic jacket that she bought when we were on a trip to Paris years earlier, and she wore it a lot.

As Liz had requested, I'd given all her clothes to her sister Margaret to divide up between her nieces. I phoned her to ask if she had kept any of them or if she'd seen the brooch.

Margaret admitted she'd kept a lot Liz's clothes. She didn't wear them, but like me with the jewellery, she couldn't part with them.

"I never saw her golden rose brooch though," she said. *"But you're welcome to look through all the clothes.'*

I went straight over to her house to sort through everything. I spotted the jacket and heaved a sigh of relief when I saw the gold rose in the lapel as I remembered.

I couldn't part with the jacket either, so I brought it with me. It's the one item of Liz's clothing which I have.

Liz's gold rose was one thing less to worry about, but I still hadn't arranged a thing for my ordination.

I decided to hold my nerve, keep the faith and wait to see what Liz and the Virgin Mary had in store for me.

I found out as soon as I called in to see my parish priest, Father Tom Dooley.

To my surprise, he revealed that he and the parish secretaries were already working on my ordination.

"Eileen and Rosemary are overseeing everything for the mass, and I'll take care of all the mass settings, readings and hymns," he said. *"It's all under control, Sean!"*

He told me that the three of them were already arranging the booklet for the ordination. They would send weekly updates to me in Rome.

They would also liaise with the diocesan office and the Bishop's master of ceremonies to sort out the finer details of the day.

All I had to do was approve and send the final copy of the booklet to the printer. I even knew the printer from my school days.

I left the parish priest's house walking on air.

Then P.J. and Joyce recommended the Heritage Hotel in Killenard for the celebration dinner that night. They booked the musical entertainment too.

They and my sisters, May and Kay, volunteered to assemble a list of all the names and addresses of our family members for the invitations.

Liz's sister Margaret said she would do the same for Liz's side of the family.

All I had to do was add the contact details of Liz's and my friends to the invitation list.

Top of my invite list was Niamh and Lorna, Liz's angels of mercy from Tallaght Hospital.

I've prayed for them every day since Liz's death and will continue to do so for the rest of my life.

I hadn't any contact with them since I'd received a card thanking me for the flowers and perfume I'd sent after Liz's funeral.

Now six years later, I called Tallaght Hospital trying to contact two nurses called Niamh and Lorna.

I didn't know their surnames at all. All I had was the date they worked there, the name of the ward and the fact that they worked the night shift.

I explained why I wanted to contact them, and a kind nurse called me back later.

"I've enquired, and I'm afraid the last we heard of Niamh is that she emigrated to Australia a few years ago," she explained.

"I've found one nurse called Lorna working here, but she's not in today, so I still don't know if she's the Lorna you're looking for."

It was the same Lorna. That week the phone rang, and I heard Lorna's sunny voice once again. She told me that Niamh moved back from Australia, and she'd contact her for me.

They both said they'd be delighted to come to my ordination.

If Liz hadn't asked me to verify Lorna's name on the morning of her death, I would have called Tallaght hospital looking for someone called Orla. I would never have been able to find them again.

Returning to Rome after the Saint Patrick's break, I had a smile on my face again. I didn't have any doubt. Liz and the Blessed Virgin, had organised everything. All I had to do was show up.

After completing the final exams, I returned home in late June and moved back into my own house.

For the remaining two weeks before my ordination, I helped out in the parish and assisted at morning mass each day as a deacon.

The church sacristan Raymond Muldowney, who's my first cousin and godchild, said he'd take care of all the flowers in the church for my ordination.

There are lots of clerics moving around the altar during an ordination, and he wanted to make sure the flowers wouldn't be in the way.

I asked him what he was planning.

"I was thinking of a large arrangement of red roses at the back of the altar and white roses in the front," he said.

I wondered if I could get some golden roses too, and I started to tell him asked him about Our Lady of The Mystical Rose.

"But I know all about the Mystical Rose, Sean!" he said.

I was amazed. I couldn't find one in fifty seminarians in the Beda, who knew anything about the Mystical Rose and my godchild knew all about her.

When he was young, he explained, his mother and mine, who were sisters, used to bring him to prayer sessions in Spink in Laois.

He got to know an elderly lady who went to the same gatherings. She prayed for priests all her life.

She told him that she was terrified of driving so, for protection, she carried a large statue of Our Lady on the front passenger seat of her car.

When she died, the old lady's brothers arrived at Raymond's house and told him she had bequeathed the statue of Our Lady to him.

It was a statue of Our Lady of the Mystical Rose.

"You can have the statue, but it's not very presentable," said Raymond. *"She had it wrapped in cling film all those years to protect it in the car.*

"I never took off the cling film because I was afraid the paint and even the plaster would come away with it."

I thought it was an amazing coincidence that he had an icon of Our Lady of the Mystical Rose. But I was firm that it was Raymond's heirloom, and I wouldn't dream of taking it.

On the week of my ordination, Raymond and his fiancee, Carmel, arrived with the statue and insisted I have it as an ordination gift. They had removed the cling film from the figure, and it was perfect with not a spot of paint missing.

Our Lady of the Mystical Rose sits on the table in my prayer room ever since as one of my favourite possessions. Liz's gold rose brooch lies in her arms.

I had no real anxiety, only excitement about my ordination.

Father Dooley, Eileen and Rosemary were the ones who did all the worrying and hard work.

Eileen and Rosemary turned my mass booklet into a work of art. They photographed the stained-glass windows in the church to decorate the brochure, so it looked like a mini-Book of Kells.

Laurence Fullam, who was our family doctor when we lived in Portarlington, was also the choirmaster. He augmented the local choir with the men's choir from the golf club and the choirs from the local parishes of Emo and Killenard.

P.J. and Joyce, May, Kay and Margaret sent out the invitations and had the hotel arrangements in place. As I suspected, all I had to do was show up.

Most Reverend Denis Nulty, the Bishop of Kildare and Leighlin, presided over an ordination ceremony filled with music, prayer and ritual.

I felt a sense of calm that day knowing that Liz and the Blessed Virgin were looking down on me, and I kept Liz's golden rose in the pocket of my vestments during the entire ceremony.

Almost all the seventy priests in active ministry in the diocese attended the ordination. Father Dooley borrowed enough chasubles - the outermost liturgical vestment - for everyone from Dublin Archdiocese for the day.

The vast procession of priests in full regalia made a solemn and beautiful spectacle.

The church and altar looked splendid as Raymond bedecked it with huge sprays of red, white and golden roses.

Saint Michael's church holds about eight hundred people, and it was standing room only that day.

Among them were my classmates Sean Nugent, Eamonn O'Connell, Chris Daly and Liam Shanahan from my days as an apprentice with the ESB.

I came to the altar holding a lighted candle, and when I was called forward, I gave the reply 'adsum', which means 'I'm present'. This was a formal expression of my acceptance of the call to serve the church.

During the prostration ceremony, I lay face down upon the floor of the altar as a sign of my unworthiness before God.

The most solemn moment of the ordination took place when the bishop laid his hands on my head. By placing his hands on me, the power of the sacrament of Holy Orders was conferred.

My sisters May and Kay had bought a white chasuble which is worn after the ordination as part of the ceremony.

People told me afterwards that their eyes filled up as they watched May and Kay help me into the priest's vestments.

P.J. and Joyce bought me a chalice, and the small plate called a paten as a gift for my ordination.

He and Margaret brought up the chalice and paten at the procession of gifts. P.J. and Margaret were the best man and bridesmaid at Liz and my wedding, and now they had witnessed my marriage to the Church.

I requested that Amazing Grace, which was one of Liz's favourite hymns, be sung after communion.

It seemed the most beautiful rendition of any hymn I've ever heard sung. To this day, to listen to it while I'm distributing Holy Communion gives me a tremendous lift.

My ordination and all the events surrounding it went like a dream. I had absolutely no doubt that Liz and the Blessed Virgin were central to it all.

More than 175 family and friends joined the celebration in the five-star Heritage Hotel in the scenic village of Killenard that evening.

Back then many of the hotels were struggling to stay in business, so we got a five-star service for three-star prices.

P.J. organised a piper, J.J. Fennelly, who was also our first cousin, to pipe the guests into the reception.

The last time I had seen him, he had piped the funeral march for Liz. Sadly, J.J. has since died himself.

Inside the hotel, P.J. had a harpist play during the pre-dinner drinks.

Liz's angels, Niamh and Lorna, had a special place of honour. So too did her treasured friends, Dolores and Mairead and the group of women from Kilcock golf club who referred to themselves as *'Liz's gang'*.

Bishop Denis, drew himself to his full height of 6' 4" to address the assembled at dinner.

He told the story about how he had gone up to the gallery before mass that day to discuss the programme with the choirmaster.

As he was coming down, he met a few of my ex-ESB colleagues and their wives ascending into the gallery.

"There are still a few seats near the front of the church where you'll get a good view of the Bishop," he advised them.

They didn't live in the area and didn't know Bishop Denis to see.

"We came to see Sean, not the Bishop!" was the reply as they continued up to the gallery.

It was a special day and a marvellous evening.

As I went to bed that night, I said: *"Liz, let the Blessed Virgin know how grateful I am. You were right; all I had to do was show up."*

Reflection with a Mystical Rose Prayer

The Mystical Rose
Blessed Mother Mary,
throughout centuries of devotion,
roses have been your symbol.

They recall for us the blossom of your love,
the freshness of your life,
and your role in bringing
newness to all things.

Help us when we see,
smell and enjoy
the gentle softness of a rose,
to understand how close
you are to us.
AMEN

My Ordination Day. From left: Monsignor John Byrne, Parish Priest of Portlaoise
& Vicar General; newly ordained Father Sean Hyland, Most Reverend Denis Nulty,
Bishop of Kildare & Leighlin; Father Tom Dooley Parish Priest of Portarlington;
and Father Tom Byrne, Parish Priest of Myshall

Our Lady of the Mystical Rose

15

My First Parish

*"Go therefore and make disciples of all nations, baptising them
in the name of the Father and of the Son and of the Holy Spirit."*
Matthew 28:19

I was an ordained priest, but I still didn't know where Bishop Denis would assign me. The Kildare and Leighlin Diocese is spread across 56 parishes in seven counties.

The dream for me was an appointment in a parish close to my hometown. That way, I could live in my own house, and start each day with the morning prayer of the Divine Office in the cemetery.

Meanwhile, my first mass of thanksgiving, the first time I'd officiate a mass, was approaching in a couple of days.

Barry Larkin, a colleague of mine in the Beda, was ordained on the same day as me in the diocese of Ferns so we couldn't attend each other's ordination ceremony.

His Mass of thanksgiving was on Monday, July 14 in Enniscorthy in Wexford. So, I scheduled mine for Wednesday, July 16 to allow us to attend each other's first mass.

Changing the schedule turned out to be a blessing as July 16 is the feast of Our Lady of Mount Carmel. I knew it was no coincidence.

St Michael's church was beautifully decked out again, and another mini Book of Kells was produced for my first mass. The church was packed to capacity.

The people of the parish are traditionally invited to a community celebration after the first mass of a new priest.

Father Dooley came to the rescue again. He volunteered the services of the parish social organiser, Julia Leavy. Julia with Marie Corcoran and the social committee arranged a memorable evening in the local GAA hall where up to 350 guests converged afterwards.

Former showband star, Louis Melia, who was a classmate of mine in 1963, provided the musical entertainment.

We had a performance of Riverdance by the local Burbage Irish Dance Academy. The line-up boasted an all-Ireland champion dancer who has since become a world champion.

To say it was a rocking evening is an understatement. I asked Liz to thank the Blessed Virgin for me, and to tell her that I now know that she keeps the best wine until last.

I was still anxious where the Bishop would post me, but I knew it wasn't appropriate to request any special consideration. I had to accept whatever appointment I got for a few years at least.

My dream was to live in my own home in Portarlington, but my hope was I'd get an appointment less than an hour's drive away.

In the end, the Bishop assigned me to the Carlow parishes of Askea, Tinryland and Bennekerry from September 1. My new home would be in Tinryland, less than an hour's drive from Portarlington.

Father Tom Little, the parish priest, phoned me five minutes later welcoming me to Tinryland.

This was followed by a call from Father Liam Morgan who I was replacing as he was moving to Naas as their parish priest. He described Tinryland as *"a little bit of heaven"*.

He talked about the house, the views, the church and the people in glowing terms. Their reassurances made leaving home a little easier.

Before moving to Tinryland, I had a brief detour to Kilcock in August. The Bishop asked me to support the now late Father P.J. Byrne the parish priest who was recovering from a small operation.

One day in late August, I arranged to meet up Father Liam in Tinryland.

He suggested that we concelebrate mass, and then he'd show me around the house and the area before he left for his new parish.

I arrived early at the church to say a prayer. I had the long white vestment called an alb over my arm. Two elderly gentlemen at the back of the church offered sound advice to this novice priest.

"Keep it short and simple," the veterans said.

I promised I'd take their advice on board.

Mondays were allocated as my day off which was perfect. It meant I could go home on Sundays after mass and visit the cemetery. Then I'd have dinner with my family and catch up on all the news on Sunday evening.

I could stay in my own house Sunday night, play golf with the seniors on Monday, visit the cemetery and return to Tinryland on Monday evening.

I thought I couldn't have asked for better.

We blitzed through the entire parish during my first week in Tinryland. It was the week before Father Tom planned to go to Lourdes.

He put his pedal to the metal to make sure we brought communion to every housebound parishioner before he left.

My first day visiting the housebound on my own didn't go as well as Father Tom's introduction.

There was no reply at the first house, and despite my best efforts, I couldn't find the second house. I lost the entire morning without managing to visit anyone.

I got out of my car at a crossroads to figure out where I was going.

I was a little sorry for myself and felt lost and lonely.

I thought: *"I know no one here, and nobody knows me."*

Then I heard the chirpy voices of school children coming up the road.

I had visited the First Holy Communion classes in Tinryland National School a few days earlier.

I could hear them in the distance saying: *"Oh look, there's Father Sean!"*

They started waving and calling out greetings of: *"Hello, Father Sean!"*, *"Hi Father Sean!"* and *"How are you, Father Sean?"* They were in no doubt that I was their priest and that they knew me, and I knew them.

Jesus couldn't have done it better if he had sent a host of angels from heaven to assure me I was on the right path and in the right place.

Needless to say, the rest of the day went like a dream.

All the parishioners and clerics across the three communities were welcoming and encouraging.

As a priest, I got to be with parishioners during their happiest times like baptisms, confirmations and weddings.

But I was also called to support and console during their darkest hours of illness and death.

I was still new to the parish when tragedy struck, as four young local women died in a horror road crash in early 2015.

Ashling Middleton, Chermaine Carroll, Niamh Doyle and Gemma Nolan, all aged 19 and 20, died in a collision in Athy in Kildare.

I never experienced this scale of shock, grief and loss across an entire community.

Three of the young women were from our parish; the fourth was from the crash site in Athy.

I visited the homes and families of the three girls from our parish the next day and spent time with each family. I was new to this type of situation, but I had lots of experience of grief.

I knew that the best you can do in the situations is to be present and listen and keep listening. There's no place for offering reasons or platitudes at that moment.

Grieving people want to talk about their lost loved one or hear about them. That's all they want. We just have to be present and listen.

Father Tom, our parish priest, handled the logistics of three huge funerals in the parish. He is amazing when it comes to dealing with crises and grief.

He's also a powerhouse of energy.

One minute I'd hear he was in a Dublin hospital visiting someone, then in a Kilkenny hospital, and next day Waterford.

I was blessed to have had him as my mentor for my first three years as a priest.

I'm no longer a novice when it comes to ministering to the grief-stricken.

One of the critical roles of a priest is offering support after the loss of loved ones.

These can be times of great loneliness, anxiety and questioning. No matter how strong our faith, it can be tested to its limits during these times.

Why has it to be this way? Why does it have to be so hard? We have no easy answers to this question.

I've been to Medjugorje on many occasions, and every time, I've received some specific blessing that has got me through a difficult time.

The first time I went to Medjugorje as a priest was with a small group from the parish in September 2016.

I had the privilege of celebrating the English-speaking mass in The Church of St James one morning.

There are usually about forty English-speaking priests in the town at that time of year, so the chance of being principal celebrant is a rare honour.

While I was there, Marian Pilgrimage's local director, David Parkes, approached me to do an interview on the role of the Blessed Virgin in my life.

Then at the last minute, he had an emergency and had to cancel.

On our last day in Medjugorje, I was due to do an interview with Mary Television on the same topic. I was finishing an early lunch when David came into the restaurant with a gift to make up for cancelling the interview.

"God bless, I hope you enjoyed your pilgrimage," he said. *"I think it's a lovely photo, but I'm only the messenger."*

I was thrilled to see a photo of me celebrating mass in Medjugorje a few days earlier. I had to put on my glasses to read the many lines of text printed across on the top half of the picture.

It was the message Our Lady gave to local visionary, Mirjana Dragicevic-Soldo on September 2.

My mass took place more than two weeks later, so I don't know why this particular message was selected to appear on my photo. But this message really spoke to me.

In it, Our Lady reminds us that she understands the pain of losing a loved one.

I received great consolation upon reading it. I believe it's a message, which can provide support and comfort to all who grieve for lost loved ones.

I was so happy with this gift that it was as good as Our Lady sending me a personal letter.

It was like she let me know that she was watching over me and was pleased with my progress as a priest.

Our Lady's Message at Medjugorje, September 2, 2016

"Dear children, according to the will of my Son and my motherly love, I am coming to you, my children, but especially to those who have not yet come to know the love of my Son. I am coming to you who think of me and who invoke me. To you, I am giving my motherly love, and I am carrying the blessing of my Son. Do you have pure and open hearts, and do you see the gifts, the signs of my presence and love?

"My children, in your earthly life, be led by my example. My life was pain, silence and immeasurable faith and trust in the Heavenly Father. Nothing is by chance: neither pain, nor joy, nor suffering, nor love. All of these are graces which my Son grants to you and which lead you to eternal life.

"Of you, my Son asks for love and prayer in Him. As a mother I will teach you: to love and to pray in Him means to pray in the silence of your soul and not only reciting with your lips; it is even the least beautiful gesture done in the name of my Son – it is patience, mercy, the acceptance of pain and sacrifice done for the sake of another.

"My children, my Son is looking at you. Pray that you also may see His face and that it may be revealed to you. My children, I am revealing to you the only and real truth. Pray that you may comprehend it and be able to spread love and hope; that you may be able to be apostles of my love. In a special way, my motherly heart loves the shepherds. Pray for their blessed hands. Thank you."

The photo of me celebrating mass at in the Church of St James, Medjugorje in September 2016

Lovely Consolations Through Liz

Before the year was out, I had another consolation of faith through Liz.

On December 28, the Feast of the Holy Innocents, my sister May phoned me again.

She had been home alone that evening watching her favourite soap on television when she sensed Liz's presence in the room. Straight away, she received an internal message from Liz.

"May, I want you to phone Sean, and let him know how proud Seana and Kieran are of what their daddy is doing."

May thought to herself afterwards: *"I'm not going to phone Sean. He'll think I'm imagining things."*

She settled back down to watch TV, but she heard Liz's voice again.

Liz was never aggressive, but she could be firm if she felt you weren't listening to something she considered important.

"May, are you really not going to deliver my message to Sean?"

May said to herself: *"Okay, I'll call Sean."*

Shortly afterwards, she had second thoughts again.

"No! I'm not going to phone Sean, he'll think I'm mad."

Then she heard the disappointed tone in Liz's voice:

"May, are you not going to do what I ask?"

This time May gave in and phoned me. I would never have thought May imagined it, and her messages from Liz are like precious jewels to me.

In December 2017, May had another internal message from Liz.

I gave all my family and Liz's family a photograph of my ordination as a keepsake. It's a photograph taken outside the church of myself, Bishop Denis and the parish priest Father Tom Dooley.

May never got around to having her photo framed, so it was lying around her living room since July 2014. She said she was preparing to go out to do some early Christmas shopping with her daughter Nicola when she spotted the photograph.

She said to herself: *"I must take this with me to get framed."*

She said immediately she heard the voice of perfectionist and ever-organised Liz speaking.

"Thank you, May," she said. *" You have no idea how much that means to me."*

A Reflection on The Church in Modern Ireland

When I set off to Rome, I feared if I made it to ordination in four years, I'd return to Ireland to minister in an environment where priests would be spat upon.

As I started my journey to the priesthood in 2009, they released the Murphy Report into the sexual abuse scandal in the Catholic Archdiocese of Dublin.

That report followed only months after the publication of the Ryan Report which dealt with abuses in industrial schools.

I read the reports in the Irish Catholic every week. They contained extracts of verbatim evidence from those in charge of the Catholic Church at the time this abuse was happening.

I read the reports each week with an ever heavier and sinking heart.

I know many good priests in Ireland, who have given their entire lives in service of God and his people, who were horrified at what emerged.

It's a wonderful calling to give your life to serving God and ministering to the people of God. It can bring great joy and a huge sense of privilege.

And far from being spat upon, what I've experienced since starting my ministry as a priest in 2014 is that where ever I go, I'm welcomed.

The people who come to my masses are there because they want to be there.

When I celebrate a baptism, wedding or funeral, I am invited to do it, and people appreciate me being there to celebrate the occasion for them and with them.

When I visit the housebound, the sick, the troubled and the grieving, they're always grateful for my presence.

But I'm always mindful that in many instances, we priests are most often preaching to the choir.

There's a good reason for that.

As we're scarce on the ground, we have to prioritise and focus our attention on the faithful.

Unfortunately, as less and less people go to mass or attend the sacraments, we're reaching a smaller and smaller population.

Some priests do Trojan work with youth groups such as those involved in the John Paul II awards for example.

There are also some priests who do great work with the marginalised and the poor of our society. Fr. Peter McVerry is an excellent example of this.

But the majority of us spend the vast majority of our time taking care of the faithful few.

Time and resources are scarce, and this is our comfort zone. We have all the joy and job satisfaction which comes with being appreciated.

Venturing out to teach and preach where we're not invited and, in most cases, not particularly welcome, is a much more difficult task.

The subject of reaching out beyond our comfort zone was one I often brought up when I was studying in the Beda.

Many of the faithful have concerns for loved ones who they know may have strayed or lost their way.

These may be people who have turned their back on Catholicism after being hurt and angered by the many sins and scandals in the Church.

I try in my own small way to deal with a couple of the questions that unbelievers often raise in part 3 of this book.

But my hope and fervent prayer is that the Church produces priests who are true men of God.

And we can make up for the Church's terrible past and its earlier wrongs and find some way to reach out to all the people we've lost.

Our jobs as priests are to let everyone know the joy and peace of having God in our lives and lead everyone on the path to eternal life through Christ our Lord.

I pray that as priests, we can do more to make sure we don't leave any people behind.

16

Consolation from Kieran

"People were bringing little children to Jesus
for him to place his hands on them, but the disciples rebuked them.
When Jesus saw this, he was indignant.
He said to them: 'Let the little children come to me, and do not hinder them,
for the kingdom of God belongs to such as these.
Truly I tell you, anyone who will not receive
the kingdom of God like a little child will never enter it.'
And he took the children in his arms,
placed his hands on them and blessed them."

Mark 10:13-16

By 2016, I settled into my routine as a priest in Tinryland. I'd had lots of consolations of faith through Liz, in all sorts of ways which I've detailed in earlier chapters.

I also had that beautiful consolation and hug from Seana through Elisa in September 2013.

Something that crossed my mind and concerned me occasionally was that I had never heard from Kieran.

My little Seana was almost two when she went to heaven. She was very advanced for her age and had many lovely mannerisms.

So, I've many lovely memories of her expressions and things that she did and said.

I don't have the same lovely bank of memories of Kieran. He was still only a baby when he died.

Kieran was born March 19, 1976, a year and a week after Seana went to heaven.

We called him after our local priest, Father Kieran Byrne, who gave us so much support after Seana's death.

Seana looked like me, but from the day he was born, Kieran looked so much like Liz and her father, Tom.

He was a croupy baby who suffered with his breathing. We spent so many nights with him and bowls of steaming water.

We were always watching over him. He was on antibiotics a lot of his life for chest infections and things like that.

We tried not to get too worried, and we reassured ourselves that he was just like me. My family said I had been the same way as a child, and I'd been fine.

We were almost glad that he was fighting off illnesses.

We had this theory that Seana was too healthy as a child. We believed that she never built up any resistance or antibodies, so the first illness to strike her, killed her.

We were in our twenties and were thinking up all these sorts of positive things in an effort to control our fretting about Kieran's health.

We decided that Kieran, with all his infections, had a better chance of withstanding a severe illness.

Yes, we decided to be confident that he'd be okay. And anyway, lightning never strikes the same place twice. Isn't that the saying?

What I remember most is playing with him when I'd come in from work in the evenings. I'd take him from his playpen and place him on his rocking horse. He loved the rocking motion of that horse, and he'd laugh and squeal with delight.

I'd tell him how I was going to teach him how to play football and teach him swimming and boxing when he got a little older.

I used to hum to him all the time, and he always seemed to enjoy it even though I'm tone deaf.

He stayed in our bedroom every night, until one morning we woke and realised he was more sickly than usual.

He had a temperature and his breathing was laboured. The fear was lodged in my throat as I bundled him and Liz into the car.

We didn't know it then, but Kieran would never come home again.

We banged on Doctor Fullam's door in the town at 7.00am. He gave our baby a shot and travelled with us in the car to Portlaoise Hospital.

Straight away, they sent us to Dublin. They knew there was something seriously wrong. I was sick to my stomach following the ambulance to Temple Street Hospital.

The doctors spent two weeks trying to diagnose his illness and battling to save him.

In his last days, they concluded it was Reye's Syndrome which is a group of symptoms recognised by an Australian doctor.

They didn't know what caused it, and they had no cure for it.

It's a rare but serious condition that causes swelling in the liver and brain. It generally happens to children under two. Few survived then, and those that did were often brain-damaged.

We know now that Reye's syndrome most often affects children recovering from a cold or other viral infection. It's also associated with the use of aspirin. But the doctors knew none of that then.

Kieran died in Temple Street on Sunday, January 23, 1977, when he was only ten months old.

Because he was so young, I don't have the same amount of memories of Kieran as I do with Seana.

I often wondered if this bothered Kieran.

I'd think: *Does he understand how much I love and miss him?*

I wasn't preoccupied with these thoughts, but it did worry me at times.

In late August 2016, I watched a disturbing documentary about child victims of disasters. It was about children gassed in Syria and others who survived an earthquake in Italy.

I saw scenes of suffering children who were struggling to breathe. It triggered memories of Kieran again.

Saint John the Baptist is one of the saints I pray through every day.

Jesus said: "I tell you, among those born of women there is no one greater than John." Luke 7:28.

So, I pray to John every day, that he asks Jesus to draw my darling Liz, our children, our parents and our brothers and sisters ever closer to His presence.

It was the night of August 29, the feast of the beheading of John the Baptist, that I had a vivid dream about Kieran.

In the dream, I walked between rows of beds in a children's hospital. I walked through the wards the way visitors or dignitaries might do after a tragedy.

Suddenly, the scene changed, and I realised I was back in Temple Street hospital. And I knew I was coming to Kieran's bed.

All the emotions I had in the hospital at the time Kieran was dying came flooding back.

I could feel nausea in the pit of my stomach, the tightness in my chest, pain throbbing in my temples, the stress of absolute desperation.

Most of the two weeks that Kieran was in the hospital, they were trying to diagnose what was wrong.

They knew the brain was swelling so they'd keep him awake during the day to monitor brain activity. It was clear Kieran was in a lot of pain.

We hummed softly to him all day long, as it seemed to be the only thing that would soothe him a little. It was a terrible, terrible time.

In my dream, when I realised I was coming to Kieran's bed, I started praying: *"Jesus, please don't let me see him suffer."*

As I arrived at his bedside in dread, Kieran opened his eyes.

In all my life, despite all the beautiful and awe-inspiring experiences I've had, nothing compared to the joy, the peace and the love I experienced looking into Kieran's eyes.

I don't have enough superlatives to describe the beauty of that experience. It is beyond anything I've encountered in this world.

I don't have words to describe it. I woke up with filled with relief and happiness, and I thanked Jesus with all my heart and soul.

The words of Saint Paul, which I learnt during primary school catechism, kept going around and around in my mind.

"Eye has not seen, nor ear heard, nor has it entered into the heart of man what things God has prepared for those who love him."

The words repeated in my head for the rest of the night and every night for weeks after this experience. It was like one of those tunes that goes around in your head, and nothing will dislodge it.

What I experienced in Kieran's eyes, however, will stay in my mind forever.

It's All About Love: A Reflection

I've read or sometimes watched testimonies of near-death experiences from people who are technically dead for short periods.

These are people who are usually revived by doctors after a heart attack or some other trauma. During the period that they 'die', many report an encounter with the next life.

Sometimes it's an angel, a long-lost loved one, or even Jesus. The experiences vary, but the one thing they all mention is the feeling of being immersed in a love and a light that's beyond description.

I often wondered how such an awesome feeling of love could be experienced in such a very brief time. Now thanks to my consolation from Kieran, I know.

I recall reading one near-death experience of a middle-aged American who had lapsed from his faith.

He didn't think he was a bad man; he hadn't done anything evil but admitted he never considered God in his life. He was wrapped up in his material world.

He said he died of a heart attack and wound up in front of Jesus. The Lord told him that due to his lifestyle, he was bound for a sweltering place.

"I understand and accept that," the man told Jesus. *"It's what I deserve. But I'm still begging you for mercy and to give me a second chance."*

Jesus relented and gave him a second chance.

The man explained: *"He told me He was sending me back to earth, but I must spend my life spreading the word that God and heaven and hell are real, and people need to repent and prepare."*

The man said he was relieved and delighted to have a second chance until he realised he had a problem.

Never having been diligent about his faith, he told Jesus, he didn't know what he should preach.

"What do I say? How do I explain this? What will I tell them it's all about?"

Jesus responded: *"It's all about love."*

Our entire earthly journey is learning about love and how to love. All the rest is noise.

If you've followed this book, you'll have gathered how much I love Liz, Seana and Kieran and how essential they are in my life.

But we are taught as Christians that we must never place anything or anyone above the love of God in our lives.

After my consolation of faith from Kieran, I prayed to Jesus to know that I had the right balance in my life.

That I loved and honoured God above all.

I seldom visualise Liz, Seana and Kieran without seeing Jesus there. And I never think about my family without feeling a great gratitude and love for Jesus.

But still, I worried about balance.

It took a while, but prayer gave me some insight and some comfort.

I thought about how we are all channels of God's love and how every person on this earth is born to be a channel of God's love.

But we have to remember a channel is merely the pipe that conducts energy, water or electricity. The pipe is never the source of what it carries, it's only the channel.

There are good channels, bad channels, great channels and poor channels.

Channels get blocked all the time. Many operate at a tiny percentage of their potential.

When we practice living the Virtues and the Beatitudes, which I wrote about at the end of Chapter 11, we are doing what we were sent here to do. We are radiating love, and it's all about love.

I realised the love I feel for Liz, my children, my parents, my brothers and sisters is God's love.

And that even the very best channel can only transmit a tiny percentage of the love of God. Our love is a pale reflection of the tremendous love God has for each one of us.

Every once in a while, God gives us a glimpse of how great this love is. When he does, we don't have the words to describe it.

Even in his last precious hours, Jesus opens his heart to His Apostles about love.

He only has a short time left on earth to impart the most important lessons he can. And one of his main lessons is about love.

He knows that he faces a painful, cruel, humiliating death but in his farewells, he gave them a new commandment - to love each other.

He said: *"Little children I shall be with you only a little longer. I give you a new commandment. You must love one another as I have loved you. It is by your love for one another that everyone will recognise you as my disciples."* John 13.33

We know that God the Father loves each of us personally. The Gospel according to John 3:16 says: *"For God so loved the world that he gave his one and only Son, that whoever believes in him shall not perish but have eternal life."*

It's all about love. From the first moment of our existence, there's love. The baby in the womb is there from love. The first time a mother lays eyes on her child, there's love. Children can't survive without love. People die without love.

God put us on the planet to love. Our Lord has commanded us to love Him: *"Thou shalt love the Lord thy God with thy whole heart, and with thy whole soul, and with thy whole mind, and with thy whole strength";*

But God also commands us to love everyone around us. God himself is Love.

And one of the great things about God's love for each one of us is that once we feel it, it banishes fear from our lives.

When we have fear in our lives, we exude anger, arrogance, impatience, greed and envy.

But once we have love in our lives, all that flows is justice, temperance, prudence, fortitude and peace of mind.

Love takes away fear. Once we feel we're in God's hands, it transforms our lives forever.

Saint Paul tells us: *"Love is patient, love is kind. It does not envy, it does not boast, it is not proud. It does not dishonour others, it is not self-seeking, and it is not easily angered. Love lasts forever and never fails."* 1 Corinthians 13:4

He also said: *"Three things will last forever - faith, hope, and love - and the greatest of these is love."* 1 Corinthians 13:13

Saint Paul says God's love conquers all, even death.

And Saint John says: *"Whoever believes in Him shall not perish but have eternal life."* John 3:16.

Since the consolations of faith that I've experienced through Liz, Seana and Kieran, I have no doubt about eternal life.

Somehow, through God's Grace, my family have been allowed to reach me and let me know they're close to me, so neither have I any doubt about eternal love.

And it's all about love.

17

Moving Home

"My people will live in peaceful dwelling places, in secure homes, in undisturbed places of rest."
Isaiah 32:18

The first year in the parishes of Askea, Tinryland and Bennekerry was a busy one. I focused on gaining experience as a priest in both the liturgical and pastoral sense.

Everything was new to me in the beginning - daily mass, baptisms, funerals, weddings, confessions and visiting the sick.

Then I had the special events like Christmas, the Easter ceremonies, First Holy Communion, and Confirmation to learn about.

By the time I started my second year, I was more assured about my work as a priest.

But I was also aware that I was growing more unsettled. I yearned to visit St Michael's cemetery in my hometown every day. I found real peace praying in the graveyard, and the desire to spend more time there was affecting my energy and motivation.

I wanted to get back to Portarlington. I was dwelling on it a lot but trying not to get depressed about it.

Bishop Denis reassigns priests once a year during August. So, I approached him in February 2016 requesting a move closer to Portarlington as soon as he could facilitate it.

The Bishop does his best to keep everyone happy. He was open to my request, but due to deaths, retirements and the ill health of some priests that year, he admitted he couldn't move me in 2016.

He reassured me that there would be changes taking place in neighbouring parishes that might suit me the following year.

As the year progressed with more deaths and early retirements from illness, it seemed to me that a move was looking less and less possible. It looked like it might be years before I'd get moved.

I pray for and to Liz all the time, but I seldom ask her for anything for myself. I know that she does all she can to intercede for me and to support and encourage me. So, I try not to burden her with further requests.

But as we moved into 2017, it seemed circumstances were conspiring against any move for me. I could see that no matter what the Bishop did, it would be difficult for him to facilitate a move for me.

Despite my best efforts, I started to feel depressed, and my energy dimmed.

Feeling desperate, I pleaded with Liz to intercede with the Blessed Virgin and Jesus so that the Holy Spirit would help.

I knew Bishop Denis would do all he could, but I realised even he might need some assistance.

I hardly dared hope when he called me in June 2017 to meet him in the Bishop's House in Carlow.

I was relieved when he revealed he had a proposal that he believed might meet my needs.

The Bishop explained that Father Greg Corcoran needed the support of a curate in the parishes of Rhode and Clonbullogue in County Offaly.

Father Greg lived in the parish house in Rhode, but he had a half hour's trip each way to get to and from the other parish.

In a perfect world, there would be a curate living in Clonbullogue too, but there was no parish house available.

Clonbullogue has its own church, and two others in Walsh Island and Bracknagh. Each village also has its own primary school.

My hometown sits a ten-minute drive to Walsh Island and Bracknagh and a fifteen-minute journey to the church in Clonbullogue.

The estate I live in is also on the outskirts of the town, on the road out to Clonbullogue, so I have no town traffic to contend with.

They realised that the house was well-located to support the needs of all three churches.

Father Greg's parish churches in Rhode and Croghan are still an easy twenty-five minute drive away.

Once again, my prayers were answered.

My dream was to live in Portarlington in my own house and minister in a neighbouring parish close by. I didn't necessarily want to minister in Portarlington.

If I sat down to write the ideal living situation for me and the place where I would minister, I couldn't have come up with a better plan.

God bless and thank Bishop Denis, Liz and the Blessed Virgin.

As I've explained in earlier chapters, I moved back to Portarlington after Liz died and bought my house in Pine Villa in 2009.

It's a bungalow in a small mature estate which is well maintained by the residents. My house is a detached three-bedroom property built about twenty-five years ago.

A family occupied the house for years before me, so when I moved in, it was clean, but well-worn.

But at that time, I was barely coping after the loss of Liz, and then I started studying for the priesthood.

So, I changed nothing.

I didn't even give it a lick of paint. I never unpacked all that Liz and I accumulated over forty years together. I stuffed anything I didn't need for day-to-day living into spare rooms or cupboards.

Then I went to Rome for four years.

Within a month of returning to Ireland for good, I moved to my first appointment in Askea, Tinryland and Bennekerry.

So, still, I did nothing to turn this house into my home.

In Liz's last days, we discussed what I'd do with possessions like her car, watch, clothes and jewellery.

Afterwards, she said: *"It's funny, but what I most wonder about is what will happen to all my kitchen and household things?"*

By this, she meant her kitchen utensils, glassware, crockery and chinaware and all the paintings, photographs and ornaments she collected.

Liz was a great cook and a perfectionist in all things, but especially in anything to do with the house.

She was a domestic diva before the phrase was even invented.

We did lots of entertaining both personal and work-related, and Liz kept the best of everything in her kitchen. But she knew all too well that I didn't cook.

I did my best to reassure her.

"Don't worry about that, Liz," I said. *"Wherever I am, everything in our house will be with me."*

We said no more on the subject. As a result of that conversation, I couldn't even give away a spoon that belonged to her.

Yet it didn't seem right that it was all lying unused in boxes in spare rooms.

My family were delighted with the news of my transfer to the parish of Rhode and Clonbullogue.

P.J. made an immediate decision.

"I'm going to redecorate and refurbish your house, the way Liz would have done it," he said.

My brother has a motor factor business in the town, but over the years, he bought older properties and renovated them for rental.

He is an industrious man who always has some project on the go.

As I said before, he is very like Liz; a real perfectionist. I'm a tidy person, but 'near enough', is generally okay for me. Liz and P.J. always examined every little detail.

Liz and I moved house many times over our married life. I'd generally select the location, the site, the size and budget for each home.

But when it came to the interior design of the house, Liz would walk straight past me and consult with P.J.

And now every time I need help planning something that's important to me, P.J. is the one I go to.

When I tried to decide on the headstone for Liz's grave, it was P.J. who came up with the solution. He also sorted out the purchase of my house in Portarlington.

When I worked on putting together a memorial card for Liz, I spent weeks selecting photos of her, Seana and Kieran. Then I spent more weeks trying to lay out the images and proportion them.

Only then did I send it to the printer for a final layout.

When I received the proof, I felt it was okay. I knew it wasn't great, but I knew it was the best I could do, and I was all ready to give a green light to the printer.

Then P.J. examined it and said: *"Okay, it's not bad, but you'll only do this once. Let's get a professional photographer and do it right; the way Liz would do it."*

We did, and P.J. was right. The photographer did a much better job than I could. Like the headstone, Liz's memorial card gives me a great sense of peace and solace every day.

My brother has lots of connections in the building trade with people who have worked in his home and on all his rental properties. Like him, they all have to be perfectionists in their trades.

He recruited all these guys to work on my house this time. With his eye for detail, he did a fantastic job refurbishing my house.

I had a brand new kitchen, walk-in showers, shiny new wooden floors and freshly painted walls.

He shelved a complete wall of my prayer room, to display all the books we had collected over the years.

He also got the help of a decorator called Catherine, who colour coordinated everything.

She unboxed Liz's kitchen utensils, glassware, china, paintings and photographs and put them in their proper place.

She even assembled photos into themed collages which she scattered around the house.

P.J., Joyce and Catherine told me many times that they felt Liz guided them in everything they did.

Every time they had to make a difficult decision, they stopped and asked Liz to let them know what she wanted. The answer would come to them.

As a result, every room in the house is filled with Liz's tastes and influence.

My wife knew that I was never a great listener, and I'm aware that it's one of my deficits.

There were times when I wouldn't listen to her, and I'd be determined to go my own way. If it wasn't important to Liz, she'd shrug and let it go.

But when it was an important issue for her, and I wasn't listening, she'd go straight to P.J. who'd invariably agree with her.

Then they both worked on me until they brought me around to Liz's way of thinking.

They always worked well together. I look at the rooms in my house, and I know that some things never change.

18

Thoughts, Prayers & God's Time

"I will give thanks to you, Lord, with all my heart;
I will tell of all your wonderful deeds."
Psalm 9:1

Father Paddy Byrne was one of the priests I consulted when I felt the call to publish this book.

Paddy had published a lovely book called *"All Will Be Well"*. In his introduction, Paddy states the reason he published his book *"was to help people in their daily journey"*.

Reading Paddy's book was one of the reasons I was inspired to write this book.

He was the first person I asked to read my first draft and to help me decide if I should publish my experiences. He couldn't have been more supportive and encouraging.

He suggested that I include a few of the Psalms and readings that resonate with me.

He said too that I should give a list of the principal prayers I recite and provide some insight into how I pray.

I'd like to sincerely thank Father Paddy for his request. I enjoyed writing this section at least as much as any other part of this book.

It happens I'm writing it on Liz's birthday, March 4, 2018. God bless you, Paddy.

My prayers will differ little from those of other priests.

We all have our central core of formal prayers, but most will have their own personal prayers of intercession and thanksgiving.

In our first year at the Beda, an old Benedictine monk gave us memorable advice. He said that you should regard prayer-time as the time you owe to God.

Because sometimes even the most devout person gets disheartened.

Mother Teresa of Calcutta in her journals admitted that in the last fifteen years of her life she found no consolation in prayer at all.

And on the days when you're distracted, or you feel you're not getting a return for your efforts, you're more likely to persist when you know it's not your time.

It's crucial that you actually give prayer a time and a place in your life.

As my Benedictine friend said, it's time you owe to God.

It's God's time.

The Breviary

When I first felt a calling to the priesthood, Bishop Jim Moriarty suggested that I meet with Father P.J. Madden.

Father P.J. lived in Graiguecullen in Carlow. He had studied for the priesthood in America after his wife died, and he had just returned to Ireland when I met him.

One of the best pieces of advice he gave me was to buy a Breviary.

I bought my own copy that week and from then started to say the Morning Office at our family graveside. My Breviary has profound significance for me now.

The Breviary, also called the Liturgy of the Hours, is the official guidebook to prayer for priests.

It contains the Divine Office - a set of Catholic prayers which priests and religious orders are obligated to say every day at stated times of the day.

Within the pages of the Breviary are of Psalms, readings, prayers and hymns.

I say the Divine Office every morning, at mid-day, during the evening and at night. As I do so, I'm conscious that I'm joining in prayer with thousands of priests and religious in monasteries, convents and churches all around the world.

The Divine Office is essential to participation in the priesthood of Jesus Christ.

The following are some of my favourite words of worship from my Breviary.

This is one I like to read when I'm at our family graveside. It's attributed to the Irish-born St. Columba also known as Columcille, Colum and Columbus (521-597).

A Favourite Morning Prayer: Alone with None but Thee

Alone with none but thee, my God,
I journey on my way.
What need I fear when thou art near,
O King of night and day?
More safe am I within thy hand,
than if a host should round me stand.

My destined time is known to thee,
and death will keep his hour;
did warriors strong around me throng,
they could not stay his power:
no walls of stone can man defend
when thou thy messenger dost send.

My life I yield to thy decree,
and bow to thy control

in peaceful calm, for from thine arm
no power can wrest my soul.
Could earthly omens e'er appal
a man that heeds the heavenly call?

The child of God can fear no ill,
his chosen dread no foe;
we leave our fate with thee, and wait
thy bidding when to go.
'Tis not from chance our comfort springs.
thou art our trust, O King of kings.

A Favourite Night-time Prayer and Hymn: Abide with Me

Abide with me: fast falls the eventide;
the darkness deepens; Lord, with me abide.
When other helpers fail, and comforts flee,
Help of the helpless, O abide with me.

Swift to its close ebbs out life's little day;
earth's joys grow dim, its glories pass away.
Change and decay in all around I see.
O Lord who changes not, abide with me.

I need your presence every passing hour.
What but your grace can foil the tempter's power?
Who like yourself my guide and strength can be?
Through cloud and sunshine, O abide with me.
I fear no foe with you at hand to bless,

though ills have weight, and tears their bitterness.
Where is death's sting? Where, grave, your victory?
I triumph still if you abide with me.

Hold now your Word before my closing eyes.
Shine through the gloom and point me to the skies.
Heaven's morning breaks and earth's vain shadows flee;
in life, in death, O Lord, abide with me.

The Psalms

The Psalms are a great source of consolation because no matter what calamity befalls us, the authors have been there and experienced them already.

There's a Psalm suitable for every mood, every tragedy and every event known to man.

The Psalms are the best known and treasured of all the books in the Old Testament and are a fundamental part of the Divine Office.

More than half of the Psalms, a collection of prayers and hymns about God, are written by King David.

Meanwhile, his son, King Solomon, was the author of the Book of Proverbs which are wise sayings that offer practical advice for people.

On a lighter note, one of my lecturers in the Beda, Father James Downey, a renowned scholar in Scripture, recites a humorous ditty which doubles as a learning device about the two Biblical kings. He says in an article in the Beda Review that he uses it 'to sex up' his course on Wisdom Literature:

King David and King Solomon Led merry, merry lives,
With many, many lady friends
And many, many wives.
But when old age crept over them

With many, many qualms,
King Solomon wrote the Proverbs
And King David wrote the Psalms.

King David wrote 73 of the collection of 150 Psalms which contain four kinds of prayer: adoration, contrition, thanksgiving and supplication.

Psalms are collective prayers and should be recited in public to have full effect. Even when someone recites the psalms on their own, they should be aware of the collective that is the Catholic Church and the brotherhood of man.

The Psalms urge us to accept situations and to accept that not everything can be solved.

And acceptance requires faith.

Psalms spoke to my heart in those early days after Liz's death, and they continue to have special resonance in my prayer life. Psalms is a beautiful book to turn to for encouragement and healing words:

A Favourite Prayer of Thanksgiving: Psalm 100
"Shout for joy to the Lord, all the earth.
Worship the Lord with gladness; come before him with joyful songs.
Know that the Lord is God.
It is he who made us, and we are his;
we are his people, the sheep of his pasture.
Enter his gates with thanksgiving and his courts with praise;
give thanks to him and praise his name.
For the Lord is good and his love endures forever;
his faithfulness continues through all generations."

A Favourite Prayer in Times of Stress:
Psalm 23, The Lord Is My Shepherd

The Lord is my shepherd; I shall not want.
He makes me lie down in green pastures.
He leads me beside still waters.
He restores my soul.
He leads me in paths of righteousness
for his name's sake.

Even though I walk
through the valley of the shadow of death,
I will fear no evil, for you are with me;
your rod and your staff,
they comfort me.

You prepare a table before me
in the presence of my enemies;
you anoint my head with oil; my cup overflows.
Surely goodness and mercy shall follow me
all the days of my life,
and I shall dwell in the house of the Lord forever.

The Mass

My prayer routine consists of daily mass. Mass is a Divine privilege for me, and when I have no public mass, I say a private one in the prayer room in my house.

Adoration of the Blessed Sacrament and prayer in front of it is another great honour. To have prayed in front of the blood and flesh of Jesus in Lanciano in Italy was another great privilege in my life.

Divine Mercy Chaplet

Reciting the Divine Mercy Chaplet is an integral part of my life and part of my daily routine at 3.00pm since 2003. Jesus made wonderful promises to Saint Faustina for the soul who is faithful to the Divine Mercy devotion.

Divine Mercy – 3.00pm Prayer

You expired, Jesus, but the source of life gushed forth for souls,
and the ocean of mercy opened up for the whole world.
O Fount of Life, unfathomable divine mercy,
envelop the whole world and empty yourself out upon us.
O blood and water which gushed forth from the heart of Jesus,
as a fount of mercy for us, I trust in you.

Divine Mercy Prayer - Chaplet

Recited in the format of the Rosary, meditating on the sorrowful mysteries.

Eternal Father we offer you the body and blood soul and divinity
of your dearly beloved Son our Lord Jesus Christ in atonement for our sins
and the sins of the whole world.
(Once first for five decades like the Our Father)

For the sake of his sorrowful passion, have mercy on us and on the whole world.
(Recited ten times for five decades like the Hail Mary)

The Rosary

I have a CD with all the decades of the Rosary which I play as I drive. Since Liz went to heaven, I try to recite the Rosary when I go to bed at night. Our Lady has made many beautiful and consoling promises to those who are faithful to the daily recitation of the Rosary.

Personal Prayers

I have many private intercessory prayers through the Blessed Virgin and many saints. These include praying for the repose of the souls of all the deceased members of my family and Liz's.

I also pray for all those who supported Liz and me as they journeyed through this life, and those who've asked for my prayers for their loved ones.

My prayers are also for the health, peace of mind and the consolations of faith for all my family and Liz's, our extended family and all their friends.

I also pray for the protection of the unborn, for the conversion of sinners and for the leadership of the Church.

My Own Prayer to my Guardian Angel

Guardian Angel, intercede for and guide me.

That I may put aside all irrational fears, anxieties and desires and focus on doing the best I can as a priest each day, to fulfil the will of The Father and the desires of Jesus in a calm, focused and diligent way.

Then let me be at peace, to leave the outcomes and the unfolding of the future in the hands of Our Father believing and accepting that Jesus can and will turn all things to the good.

I pray for the grace to treat all people I meet with compassion, caring and love, and never with impatience, arrogance or anger.

My Own Prayer of Thanksgiving

I thank Jesus for the presence of Your Blessed Mother in my life and for her lovely and awesome supports and consolations.

I thank You for the precious gift of my darling Liz, Seana and Kieran and Aine; for my father and mother and sisters and brother; also for the friends and relations who have supported me, Liz and our families; and for all those who continue to help us during their journey on earth.

I thank You for all the priests and religious who have supported and continue to help me in my ministry as a priest.

A Favourite Reading from Isaiah 43:1-5

The Lord who you created says
"Do not fear, for I have redeemed you;
I have summoned you by name;
you are mine.
When you pass through the waters,
I will be with you;
your troubles will not overwhelm you.
When you pass through the rivers
They will not sweep over you.
When you walk through the fire,
You will not be burned;
The hard trials that come will not hurt you.
For I am the Lord your God, the
Holy One of Israel, who saves you.
I will give up whole nations to save your life,
Because you are precious to me
And because I love you and give you honour
Do not be afraid I am with you."

A Short Prayer from Saint Thomas Aquinas

"Grant me, O Lord my God, a mind to know you, a heart to seek you, wisdom to find you, conduct pleasing to you, faithful perseverance in waiting for you, and a hope of finally embracing you. Amen"

Thoughts as Prayers

The philosopher Plato said: *"A person comes to resemble that which they continually contemplate."*

Over the years, I observed what Plato says in the way Liz lived her life. She thought peaceful, loving thoughts and her actions were peaceful and loving as a result.

She would never stay in the company of people where bitter words or malicious gossip was being exchanged on for example. She wouldn't lecture, hector or be disruptive but she'd try to change the conversation to a happier topic. And if she didn't succeed, she'd slip away and play with children, or admire the flowers or the stars.

We should always remember that our thoughts become our words, our words become our actions, and our actions generate reactions.

Our thoughts can define our reality.

If we start the day with well-meaning, positive and happy thoughts, our first words are likely to be well-meaning and happy, and so is the reaction we get from those around us.

Just as if we start our day with frustration, bitterness or angry, our words will follow and so will the reactions we receive.

So, it follows that we should try to let our thoughts become our prayers, and our prayers become our thoughts.

Positivity as Prayer: Seeing Heaven from Here

When I was general manager of an American company in Ireland in the 90s, I liaised with a colleague in the U.S.

As director of manufacturing, he had responsibility for a large contract making machines in Mexico.

It was a nightmare for him. The contract was always behind schedule, over-budget and always had severe quality-control problems.

When I'd call him to enquire how things were going, he had a response that made me laugh.

"It ain't hell, but I can see it from here."

To paraphrase my old friend, for me, *life ain't heaven, but I can see it from here.*

I know the Blessed Virgin, Jesus, Liz and our children are close to me and watching over me all the time.

My understanding of theology is that when we die and go to heaven, we can request special graces for our loved ones in purgatory or on earth.

And that's how I choose to interpret the amazing consolations and encouragement I've received. They are the result of intercessions by Liz, Seana and Kieran in heaven.

It may not precisely be church teaching on how it all works, but I believe that Liz, through the Virgin Mary and Our Lord, tries to ensure that I'm safe and happy.

Once Liz arrived in heaven to be reunited with our children, parents and brothers and sisters, I know her next thought would be for me.

She would ask Jesus: *"Please Jesus, give me a little time to take care of Sean."*

Love is the premier currency in heaven and on earth. When Jesus sees unconditional love, he won't stand in the way.

I am only half-joking when I tell friends that Liz is beavering away in heaven earning graces for me. And she has Seana and Kieran beavering away with her.

Whenever Liz sees I'm in need, she goes to the Blessed Virgin with that mischievous glint in her eye, and she asks Mary to make the request to Jesus.

When Jesus sees his mother coming after talking with Liz, he says:

"Now Mother, you know we love her dearly, and we love Sean. But I have a whole universe to take care of. If I keep letting her send these messages and supports, I'll have a billion people outside my door in the morning who'll want to do the same."

Then Mary says: *"Ah Jesus, just wait until I tell you what she wants to do this time…"*

And Jesus never refuses his mother

We all have our own view of how it operates. That's my version, and I'm sticking to it.

Postscript

As you will have gathered from this book so far, the Blessed Virgin was central to my call to the priesthood.

Her message by way of a locution in 2003 foreshadowed all that would unfold in our lives.

Then the date that Bishop Denis choose for my ordination turned out to be the Feast of the Mystical Rose. In the unfolding events leading up to my ordination, I was left in absolutely no doubt that this was not just a coincidence.

One of the key influences in choosing to try and launch Whisperings of My Soul for Christmas 2018 was Liz's 10th anniversary.

I passionately wanted to acknowledge the ongoing role of Liz and the Blessed Virgin in my life and my ministry.

When I realised in spite of a number of rejections from publishers, that I could accomplish this, it seemed like my prayers were answered.

When Bishop Denis agreed to preside at the launch, and I could get it launched in time for the Christmas market, it seemed like heaven was truly smiling on the project.

I left for a week in Medjugorje on October 3rd with the announcement for the launch on November 30th appearing in all the parish weekly newsletters the next week end.

It looked like the book was set for a successful launch.

I arrived back from Medjugorje on October 11th to hear RTE had announced the Late Late Toy Show for November 30th. My heart sank a little.

I met my brother P.J. the next day to discuss the design of a poster announcing the launch. He confirmed my worst fears and thought the potential attendance at the launch would be dramatically reduced by the clash with Late Late Toy Show.

I went to bed with a slightly sick feeling in the pit of my stomach.

All I could muster as a prayer was, "*Liz I hope you and the Blessed Virgin are working on something that I cannot see, because it does not look good to me.*"

It seemed improbable that I could get another date from

Bishop Denis that would align with the venue being available in time for a pre-Christmas release.

The next day, I emailed Bishop Denis with the request for an alternative date that he would be available. He phoned within an hour to say he would be available on Friday December 7th, alerting me that it was the eve of the Feast of The Immaculate Conception of the Blessed Virgin Mary, in case I would have commitments for vigil masses.

I knew immediately what Liz and the Blessed Virgin were working on.

Julia confirmed that the venue was available December 7th. So, the re scheduled launch date became Friday, December 7th the eve of the Feast of the Immaculate Conception of the Blessed Virgin Mary.

It all fell into place as I hoped and prayed. There's a form of prayer in positivity and looking on the bright side of life.

As I've said, my life ain't heaven, but I can see it from here!

PART TWO

MIRACLES - OUR JEWELS OF FAITH

"He performs wonders that cannot be fathomed,
miracles that cannot be counted."
Job 5:9

Miracles – Our Jewels of Faith

Introduction

In part 1 of this book, I write about the many small, personal miracles that have graced my life and provided great consolation to me during the most difficult times of my life.

These consolations of faith have served as quiet assurances that God is watching out for me and always helping me.

But in this part of the book, I want to explore the many other times when God reveals His great power and mercy in much greater ways.

Miracles are signs of God and are precious jewels in our huge tapestry of faith.

Through many of His extraordinary miracles, he has inspired believers throughout the ages and all around the world to deeper faith and devotion.

These miracles are the equivalent of flashing neon signs pointing in the direction of God.

Each of them is a reminder that nothing is impossible when it comes to God. They help to console us, to find fortitude and to renew our faith in times of trial and sorrow.

They demonstrate how real God is; how close he is to us; how much Jesus Mary and all the inhabitants of heaven care about us and are constantly seeking ways to help, encourage and support us in our life's journey and our daily struggles.

Through His miracles, God gives believers and those doubting their faith a little extra help.

Many have tried to prove these miraculous phenomena are nothing more than deceptions and hoaxes.

Yet despite modern investigations, they remain inexplicable to scientific and natural laws.

I want to explore just three of those jewels of faith that I am particularly drawn to and have great personal attachment to.

For me and other believers, they provide more irrefutable evidence of God revealing Himself to us in this world.

The Eucharistic Miracle of Lanciano

Introduction to the Miracle of Lanciano

After Liz and I lost Seana and Kieran, all our holidays became pilgrimages.

We figured that anything that brought us closer to heaven, to where God was and where our children were, was where we wanted to be.

We went to Lourdes, Fatima, the Holy Land and made plans to go to many other places.

One of the places at the top of our list to visit after I retired was Lanciano in Italy.

The Eucharistic Miracle of Lanciano called out to both of us.

This was the first and most famous of Eucharistic Miracles and has artefacts all validated by scientific investigation.

We both also have a great devotion to Pope John Paul II and he visited the shrine in 1974 when he was Cardinal of Krakow, Karol Wojtila.

The Pope imparted an apostolic blessing to the people of Lanciano-Ortona in 2004 and said: *"For us Christians the Eucharist is our all: it is the centre of our faith and the source of all our spiritual life."*

As I've related earlier, Liz fell ill and died before we ever got to make our planned journey to Luciano.

A few years later, I managed to make the trip for both of us, the story of which I relate below.

The Miracle

In ancient times, the order of Saint Basil monks fled persecution in Greece and took refuge in a place now known as Lanciano in Italy.

The hill-top Roman trading town, then known as Anxanum, was the original birthplace of Saint Longinus - the centurion who pierced Jesus with his spear during the crucifixion

After the crucifixion, Longinus is said to have quit the Roman army, converted to Christianity and died later as a martyr.

The Greek monks built a monastery in honour of Longinus in the Roman town.

In honour of Longinus and the Eucharistic miracle which took place in his church, the city became known as Lanciano, which translates as 'The Lance'.

We have no exact date for the Eucharistic Miracle of Lanciano, but it is said to have taken place sometime between 730 and 750A.D.

It happened while a Basilian monk, whose name has been lost in the annals of time, celebrated mass in the church.

Like many of his order, he was probably Greek and an ancient document from the 1600s described him as "*versed in the sciences of the world but ignorant in that of God.*"

The monk was having a crisis of faith and had recurring doubts about the presence of God in the Eucharist.

As he performed the consecration, he witnessed the host of leavened bread transform into flesh, and he saw the red wine turn into blood.

Excerpts from a document kept at Lanciano read:

"*Frightened and confused by so great and so stupendous a miracle, he stood quite a while as if transported in a divine ecstasy.*"

Finally, he recovered and with his face streaming with tears, he called the congregation to come to the altar and witness the miracle themselves:

"Oh fortunate witnesses to whom the Blessed God, to confound my unbelief, has wished to reveal Himself in this Most Blessed Sacrament and to render Himself visible to our eyes.

"Come Brethren, and marvel at our God so close to us. Behold the Flesh and the Blood of our Most Beloved Christ."

The congregation, who were reportedly *'completely terrified'*, spread world of the miracle throughout the land.

Shortly after the miracle, the blood coagulated into five globules of different sizes. The circle of flesh remained as it was with a piece of the original leavened bread still at its centre.

It is claimed that the Church authorities certified the miracle, but the original document was lost some time in the 16th century.

The Order of Saint Basil held custody of the relics until 1176 when they were handed into the care of the Benedictines.

In 1252, the relics came under the care of the Franciscans.

By now it was 500 years since the miracle, and the Church of Saint Longinus was tumbling from earthquake damage and crumbling with age.

The monks completed a new Church of Saint Francis or San Francesco in 1258 in honour of Saint Francis of Assisi.

The relics have been on display in this basilica ever since and are still under the care of the Franciscans.

In 1574, Archbishop Antonio Gaspar Rodríguez ordered an investigation into the miracle.

Eight hundred years had passed since the miracle took place, and the Church noted there was no visible sign of deterioration in the relics.

The flesh was uncorrupted and the blood remained as it was for centuries.

The investigation also included the weighing of the globules of blood which were all different sizes.

The Archbishop and other witnesses claimed that each globule of blood weighed the same as the other, and any combination of them or all five together also weighed the same.

That phenomenon has never been witnessed since then.

An inscription on the right-hand side of the Church of Saint Francis announces the "recognition" of the Holy Relics on February 17th, 1574.

In the early centuries, the flesh and blood were held in an ivory reliquary.

In 1713, it was replaced by the gold-plated silver and crystal reliquary which we still see today in the Church of Saint Francis.

The circle of flesh is displayed on top in what's called a monstrance.

These ornamental cases have windows to display the consecrated host during processions and devotional ceremonies.

The flesh is roughly the same size as the large communion wafer used today in the Latin church. Light brown in colour, it appears rose-coloured when lit from the back.

The globules of blood are held in a crystal chalice which is attached to the bottom of the monstrance.

Some believe the crystal is part of the original 8th century chalice used by the monk who witnessed the Eucharistic miracle.

The blood is described as having the colour of yellow ochre.

The Science

Pope Paul VI gave a green light to conduct the first modern study of the relics in 1970.

Doctor Odoardo Linoli, who conducted the study, was an eminent Italian professor of anatomy and pathological histology, chemistry and clinical microscopy.

He was also the former head of the Laboratory of Pathological Anatomy at the Hospital of Arezzo.

He was assisted by Doctor Ruggero Bertelli, professor emeritus of human anatomy at the University of Siena who independently corroborated the findings.

Doctor Linoli presented his findings on March 4th, 1971.

He concluded that the flesh in the reliquary was myocardium or muscular tissue from a human heart.

He reported that the blood is from a human too, and both relics belong to the same blood type AB. This is one of the rarest blood types in Europe but more common in the Middle East.

The blood-type is identical to that which Professor Baima Bollone uncovered in the Holy Shroud of Turin.

Doctor Linoli found proteins in the same proportions found in the make-up of normal blood.

The professor denied any claims that the blood could have been taken from a cadaver as he says it would have deteriorated rapidly.

There was no sign of salt or other preservatives in the tissue.

Remarkably, the samples had not decomposed or deteriorated despite being free of preservatives, and being left open to air, bacteria and light.

However, the centre of the host, the only part that had remained as the monk's original leavened bread, had entirely decayed.

Moreover, the doctors both concluded that only the skill of a trained pathologist could have obtained the sample from the heart.

The skilled cross-section contains the myocardium, the endocardium, the vagus nerve and also the left ventricle of the heart.

Professor Bertelli confirmed that the first anatomical dissections on the human body did not even begin taking place for another 600 years in Europe.

The detailed cross-section of the heart is remarkable considering pathology did not begin emerging as a scientific field until the Italian Renaissance in the 14th century.

My visit to Lanciano

During the four years that I was in the seminary in Rome, I never travelled anywhere except to go home to Ireland.

We got breaks in the semester on average every five weeks, and I flew straight home every time to go the cemetery.

I played a bit of golf as well, but mostly I wanted to visit the cemetery.

Each year in June, students who completed year three were ordained as deacons.

The rest of the seminarians finished for the summer the week before, but we were not allowed to go home.

We all had to stay until after the ordination ceremony in the Cathedral of Saint Paul Outside the Walls.

There were no exceptions. The rector of the Beda wanted a full complement of seminarians to show their support for the deacons.

Also, they needed us to work.

The college hosted a celebration meal for the deacons and the families and friends who travelled to Rome for their ordination along with the staff and students.

The college did not have a large housekeeping staff so we were all roped in to serve the meal and to clean up that day.

The week before the ordinations, we were free to go where ever we wanted, as long as we didn't go home.

The college suspected that we could find a hundred excuses not to come back for the ordinations once we went home.

It was during that free week in my second year at the Beda, that I decided to visit the Miracle of Lanciano.

The city is on the east coast of Italy, a four-hour bus trip from Rome.

It was around noon that day when I first set eyes on the Church of St Francis, home to the miraculous relics.

The church is a simple, solemn structure standing in the Piazza Plebiscito in the heart of the town.

It glows in the sunshine with warm, golden hues from its locally-hewn limestone and is surrounded by picturesque medieval streets.

There was nothing solemn or beautiful, however, about the sight of hundreds of tourists spilling out of buses and into the piazza outside the church.

My heart sank as I saw the sheer numbers of Chinese, Japanese, American and every nationality of tourist queueing to enter the church.

When I got into the church, my heart sank even further when I saw the hordes filing past the relics.

It was so sad to see no sign of reverence or devotion. I didn't see a prayer being uttered, a bow of the head or a knee bent in genuflection.

There was no acknowledgement that this was something special, a sign of God in the world.

People just shuffled past, more concerned with clicking their cameras or capturing the image of the relics on their phones.

There was no opportunity for quiet contemplation or prayer. It was hectic in the church.

I talked with the church attendant, who warned me that they were closing in ten minutes at 12.30am and wouldn't be reopening until 3.00pm.

I gave up, and decided instead to go and check into my hotel in Lanciano.

I was determined to get back to the church and be first in the queue when the doors reopened for the afternoon.

I hoped that maybe it would be more peaceful when I got back at 3.00pm.

I arrived back well before the official opening time and waited at the door.

The attendant, who I'd been talking to earlier, spotted me outside and out of some kindness, he furtively opened the door and ushered me in.

He must have felt my anxiety and disappointment earlier.

I found myself sitting at the front of the empty chapel before the blessed relics.

They were so close, that I could have touched the reliquary that holds them.

I recited my Divine Mercy, that particular passion of mine right up to 3.00pm - the time of Christ's death on the cross.

I got to pray in the way I wanted to. I had peaceful, cool silence with my eyes fixed on the miraculous relics for fifteen glorious minutes.

Then at 3.00pm, the doors opened and all hell broke loose again.

The crowds poured in, people teemed around and the cameras started clicking again.

It didn't bother me this time. I sat there for a while and then explored the rest of the church.

The next morning when I was leaving, the church was heaving with busloads of tourists again.

I didn't care.

I didn't have a lot of time in Lanciano, but I got to do what I wanted to do. I felt so grateful.

It was like getting a message from Jesus:

"You made the effort to come here. You believed. Yes, there were busloads of tourists, but I made sure you got your fifteen minutes, didn't I?"

Lanciano is a special place, but that's what made it even more special for me.

Eucharistic Miracle of Lanciano: Flesh in the monstrance above and Globules of blood in the chalice below

The Host-flesh of the Miracle of Lanciano

(Photo credit: Taken from https://en.wikipedia.org/wiki/Miracle_of_Lanciano#/media/File:Eucharistic_Miracle_of_
Lanciano_-_rear-lighted_panel_-_front.JPG

Five globules of blood

(Photo credit: Taken from https://en.wikipedia.org/wiki/Miracle_of_Lanciano#/media/File:Eucharistic_Miracle_of_
Lanciano_-_rear-lighted_panel_-_front.JPG

Our Lady of Guadalupe

Introduction to the Miracle of Guadalupe

The Blessed Virgin is huge in my life and I've always had a special devotion to her.

I first heard about the Mexican apparitions and our Lady of Guadalupe many years ago.

We have Fatima, Lourdes, Knock and Medjugorje in Europe, but the equivalent in South America is Our Lady of Guadalupe.

It's a lovely story in itself, and the imprint of the Virgin is an object of great devotion in Mexico and beyond.

The 'tilma' or cloak that is imprinted with the image of the Blessed Virgin has captured the imagination of believers for nearly 500 years.

However, the most extraordinary secrets of Our Lady of Guadalupe have only been revealed in recent years.

And it has been modern scientific investigations that have uncovered the real wonders of the image.

The Miracle

These early Marian apparitions took place at Tepeyac near present day Mexico City around 30 years after the Spanish conquered the region.

A humble farmer and descendent of the fallen Aztec Empire was chosen to witness the miracle of Our Lady of Guadalupe.

The man, who was originally known as Cuauhtlatoatzin, took the name Juan Diego when he converted to Catholicism.

One day when he was a 57-year-old widower, he was walking near Tepeyac Hill when he came upon an apparition of a beautiful "maiden" bathed in light and surrounded by music.

The day was Saturday, December 9th, 1531 and in those days, it was the Feast of the Immaculate Conception across the Spanish Empire.

The maiden, who appeared to be wearing the dress of an Aztec princess, spoke to him in his native Nahuatl language.

Her words to Juan Diego were as follows:

"Know for certain, least of my sons, that I am the perfect and perpetual Virgin Mary, Mother of the True God through whom everything lives, the Lord of all things near and far, the Master of heaven and earth.

"It is my earnest wish that a temple be built here to my honour.

"Here I will demonstrate, I will exhibit, I will give all my love, my compassion, my help and my protection to the people. I am your merciful mother, the merciful mother of all of you who live united in this land, and of all mankind, of all those who love me, of those who cry to me, of those who seek me, of those who have confidence in me.

"Here I will hear their weeping, their sorrow, and will remedy and alleviate all their multiple sufferings, necessities and misfortunes."

Our Lady asked Juan Diego to go to the Archbishop and tell him that her name was Our Lady of Guadalupe and that she wanted a church built on this site of the apparition in Tepeyac.

This was to be the first of four apparitions that Juan would witness while his uncle would witness a fifth.

The simple peasant did as he asked but Archbishop Juan de Zumarraga, a Franciscan, dismissed the story and sent him away.

Juan returned to tell the Virgin Mary what had happened and he begged her to send someone of more importance because the Archbishop would not listen to him.

However, Our Lady asked him to return to the Archbishop again the next day. Juan returned to give the same message to the Archbishop as Our

Lady requested on Sunday, December 10.

The Archbishop sent him way again and told him not to come back until he had a miraculous sign that would prove his story.

Juan returned to the site of the apparitions and told the Virgin Mary what the Archbishop had said.

She told him to return the next day and she would provide him with a sign.

However, the next day Juan's beloved uncle, Juan Bernardino, the man who had raised him from a child, fell seriously ill.

Juan Diego never went to Tepeyac to collect the sign he needed to bring to the Archbishop's residence.

By Tuesday, December 12, his uncle was dying so he left the house to get a priest.

On his way, Juan had another apparition of the Virgin Mary and he explained that he hadn't returned to her because his uncle was ill.

The Virgin Mary gently chided him with the words:

"Am I not here, I, who am your mother? Are you not under my shadow and protection? Are you not in the hollow of my mantle, the crossing of my arms? Am I not the source of all your joy? What more do you need? Let nothing else worry you, disturb you."

The Spanish words for *"Am I not here, I, who am your mother?"* are inscribed over the door of the Basilica of Guadalupe to this day.

After being assured that his uncle would be well, Juan followed the Virgin Mary's new instructions.

She told him to go to the top of Teypeyac hill and pick the roses there.

Our Lady's request confused Juan as it was winter and the mountain was barren. But when he reached the crest of the hill, he found a bush of beautiful Castilian roses in bloom.

The roses were neither in season nor native to the region.

He arranged the flowers in his tilma, a yarn cloak made from rough agave fibre worn by the poor people of the time.

The Blessed Virgin instructed him to only open the cloak again when he reached the Archbishop.

At the same time that Our Lady was with Juan Diego, she also appeared at the bedside of his dying uncle, Juan Bernadino.

As soon as she appeared in his room, the uncle recovered. The uncle claimed that she repeated to him her message that she wanted to be known as "Our Lady of Guadalupe."

Juan Diego travelled to the Archbishop's residence with the out-of-season roses as miraculous proof that he was telling the truth.

When he got an audience with the Archbishop, he opened his cloak and the Castilian roses spilled onto the floor. What caught everyone's attention, however, was the fabric of his tilma where the incredible image of Our Lady of Guadalupe had miraculously appeared.

Our Lady was portrayed with dark hair and high cheekbones with her head bowed and her hands folded in prayer to God.

Her dark complexion and features are said to be those of a mestiza - the offspring of a Spaniard and an indigenous person.

On her blue cloak, there are scatterings of stars and under her feet is a crescent moon, a symbol of the old Aztec religion of the area.

The measurements were first recorded in 1786 and the tilma's height is 170cm or 67 inches and the fabric width is 105cm or 41 inches.

Word of the miracle spread across Mexico. Millions of indigenous people turned away from their old Aztec faith within a few years of the apparition.

Soon, more than 3,000 indigenous people were converting to Catholicism every day.

The indigenous people of Mexico were often subject to discriminatory treatment by the Spaniards, and the apparition was seen as a rebuke to the conquistadors.

For Juan Diego's people, Our Lady of Guadalupe was a sign that the Virgin and her God accepted all people.

Juan Diego moved to Tepeyac Hill beside the church built for Our Lady of Guadalupe.

He lived a solidarity life of prayer and work and died 17 years after the first apparition on December 9, 1548.

Juan was beatified on May 6, 1990 by Pope John Paul II and canonised as Saint Juan Diego Cuauhtlatoatzin on July 31, 2002.

He became the first Catholic indigenous saint from the Americas. His feast day is celebrated on December 9 and he is the patron saint of Indigenous people.

His tilma is now enshrined in the Basilica of Our Lady of Guadalupe in Mexico City.

The basilica is the most visited Catholic pilgrimage site in the world with over 20 million people worshiping at the shrine.

All pilgrims see the tilma from a moving walkway designed to keep the thousands of daily visitors in constant motion.

On December 12 of each year, the last date on which the Virgin appeared to Juan Diego, the Catholic Church celebrates the Feast of Our Lady of Guadalupe.

The Science

The true origin and nature of the "tilma" with the image of Our Lady of Guadalupe remains a mystery.

As with many miracles, scientific studies have only served to reveal more of its magnificent mysteries.

The remarkable state of preservation of the tilma is the first thing to confound those who study it.

The fabric imprinted with Our Lady of Guadalupe's image is made of maguey fibre from a succulent called Agave which is a cactus-type plants of the region.

This rough, vegetable-based traditional textile was woven and worn by indigenous people of the 16th century.

However, it has a lifespan estimated at between 20 to 50 years at the most and should have decomposed by the early 17th century.

Yet, for its first one hundred years, the Church hung it unprotected and open to the elements such as humidity and light.

The faithful also subjected it to their kisses and tears and pressed their faces to the icon during its early decades.

Despite being almost 500-years-old, it shows no signs of disintegration.

In 1979, Doctor Philip Serna Callahan, a biophysicist at the University of Florida, and an expert in infrared photography, examined the image.

He found that most of the entire painting seemed to have been done with a single brush stroke.

"The original figure, including the rose robe, blue mantle, hands and face … is inexplicable," he concluded.

He added: *"There is no way to explain either the kind of colour luminosity and brightness of pigments over the centuries."*

He was also astonished by the tilma's longevity.

"It is remarkable that after more than four centuries there is no fading or cracking of the original figure on any portion of the agave tilma, which… should have deteriorated centuries ago."

Doctor Adolfo Orozco, a researcher and physicist at the National University of Mexico, also remarked in 2009 about the remarkable preservation of the tilma.

Dr. Orozco said, he could not explain the tilma's survival after being *"exposed for approximately 116 years without any kind of protection, receiving all the infrared and ultraviolet radiation from the tens of thousands of candles near it and exposed to the humid and salty air around the temple."*

The fact it has survived two near disasters is a miracle in itself.

In 1785, a worker accidentally spilled 50% nitric acid solvent while cleaning glass around the tilma. Despite falling onto a large part of the tilma, the only burn marks that show are on parts of the fabric not bearing the image.

In 1921, an activist hid a bomb containing dynamite in a pot of roses and placed it before the image inside the Basilica at Guadalupe.

When the bomb exploded, windows were blasted into the street, the marble altar rail and floor were destroyed.

A large brass crucifix in front of the image was bent backwards with the force of the blast.

However, the tilma and its glass surrounding remained unscathed.

Other scientists have examined the stars which were apparently randomly scattered on the tilma.

Doctor Hernández Illescas, a medical doctor and amateur astronomer working with Father Mario Rojas, made an astonishing discovery when they performed an astronomical study of this star pattern in 1981.

They discovered this was no random placement. They claim the stars are aligned to recreate the constellations as they were on December 12th, 1531 at 10:26am.

This was the morning that Juan Diego opened the tilma in the Archbishop's residence.

One of the greatest mysteries of the tilma is found within Our Lady of Guadalupe's eyes.

In 1929, Alfonso Marcue, who was the official photographer of the Basilica of Guadalupe, spotted what appeared to be an image of a bearded man reflected in the right eye of the Virgin.

Others examining detailed photos of the face also discovered the bearded man and saw that he appeared in both eyes.

In March 27, 1956, Doctor Javier Torroella Bueno, an ophthalmologist saw the human figure in both eyes. He noted that the distortion of the images agree with the curvature of the cornea.

Doctor Jose Aste Tonsmann, a civil engineer from Cornell University, scanned the eyes at very high resolutions and magnified them 2,500 times.

He made the most incredible discovery of all.

Not only did the digital images reveal the "human bust" of the bearded man in both eyes. The newly enhanced photos showed a total of 13 human figures.

The same microscopic people are present in both the left and right eyes, in different proportions, as would happen when human eyes reflect the objects.

In his book *"El Secreto de sus Ojos"* (The Secret of her Eyes), he says the eyes show a snapshot of the people in the room as Juan Diego unravelled the tilma in 1531.

Tonsmann discerned a seated Indian, who is looking up to the heavens and an elderly man with a white beard, much like a portrait of Archbishop Zumárraga painted in the era.

Also present is an Indian with a beard and moustache, likely Saint Juan Diego. He believes the younger man in the image is probably an interpreter called Juan González.

Also, in the collection of people is a woman of dark complexion, possibly a Negro slave who was in the bishop's service.

It is little wonder that the images in the eyes are commonly referred to as "miraculous paintings" or "heavenly photographs."

A Reflection on Our Lady of Guadalupe

I was lucky enough to attend a retreat a few years ago where I met an indigenous Mexican who had a great devotion to Our Lady of Guadalupe.

He wasn't a theologian or a philosopher or a scientist. He was just an ordinary man and compared himself to a peasant like Juan Diego, but he devoted his whole life to learning about and studying the tilma.

He was so interested and so learned about the miracle that he was asked to give a presentation to Pope John Paul II when the pontiff visited Guadalupe in 1999.

He has an exact replica of the tilma which he uses as an aid in his presentation.

It was only the first time he'd been invited to speak at a retreat in Europe, and he was doing it in gratitude for a cure of a recent illness. His English is poor, so he made his presentation through an interpreter.

But I felt privileged to talk with him through his interpreter over lunch and listen to his knowledge of, and his passion for the tilma.

As I've said, the story is a lovely one in itself but the results of the scientific studies are incredible.

The secrets in her eyes could only ever have been discovered with modern technology. It's like Our Lady has been storing some revelations for our time.

The description of what can be seen in her eyes is just incredible. How can you refute that kind of evidence?

The studies that revealed the stars on the tilma are reflections of the constellations in 1531, are also amazing.

All these revelations continue to defy sound scientific explanation, but to me there is no doubt. The tilma is another wonder that points to God's incredible power and care for us.

I've always had a huge devotion to the Blessed Virgin but for me, Our Lady of Guadalupe is the most intriguing and wondrous Marian apparition of them all.

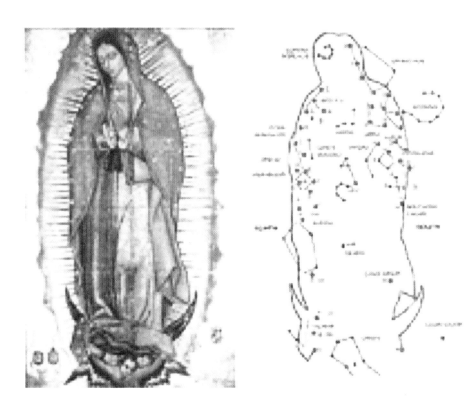

Constellations from 1531 mapped out on the tilma of Our Lady of Guadalupe

(Photo Credit: Left image of Our Lady taken from https://en.wikipedia.org/wiki/File:Virgen_de_guadalupe1.jpg. The second image is an astronomical study of the image by Father Mario Rojas and Dr. Juan Hernández Illescas on December 22, 1981 at the Observatory Laplace Mexico City.)

The Shroud Of Turin

Introduction to the Shroud of Turin Icon

The Shroud of Turin has intrigued me ever since I started searching for God.

And the Shroud, which confounds scientists from all around the world, continues to be a source of fascination for me today.

Even when radiocarbon dating in the 1980s indicated that the fabric came from the Middle Ages, I never doubted its authenticity. Soon, it emerged that the dating was faulty.

I've followed news on the Shroud through the highs and lows of scientific investigation, but I've always believed that it's the most amazing artefact related to Jesus that we've been graced with.

The Divine Mystery of the Shroud

The Shroud of Turin has been investigated by scientists for a hundred years now, yet remains the centre of huge controversy.

Some people like to consider it an ingenious hoax. However, most people revere this 4.4 metre (14.5 foot) length of ancient linen as the burial cloth of Jesus.

The linen shows the imprint of a bearded, long-haired man, naked, his arms crossed in front of him.

Both the front and the back of the man appears on the shroud. The front is on one end of the cloth and the back on the other end with the heads meeting towards the middle.

Despite exhaustive tests, scientists have never been able to explain how the imprint of the man was made.

Within the folds of the linen, there are also many blood marks which provide physical evidence of scourging, torture and crucifixion.

The Shroud's great importance is that its authentication would add credibility to the biblical account of the death and resurrection of Christ

We know there are no signs of putrefaction on the cloth so the man contained within the linen did not remain there for long.

The earliest references to Christ's burial shroud is found in the Gospels of Matthew, Mark and Luke.

The Gospels say the body of Jesus was wrapped in linen bought by a wealthy man called Joseph of Arimathea

According to Luke 23:50-53: *Now there was a man named Joseph, a member of the Council, a good and upright man, who had not consented to their decision and action.*

"He came from the Judean town of Arimathea, and he himself was waiting for the kingdom of God.

"Going to Pilate, he asked for Jesus' body. Then he took it down, wrapped it in linen cloth and placed it in a tomb cut in the rock, one in which no one had yet been laid."

For many hundreds of years after the death of Jesus, there was no mention of the Shroud.

However, a burial cloth, which some historians believe was the Shroud, is known to have been in the possession of the Byzantine emperors.

The Knights Templar were aware of this relic because a French knight, Robert of Clari, reported seeing it in 1203 in Constantinople, now modern Istanbul.

That cloth disappeared from all records after the Sack of Constantinople in 1204.

Some believe the Knights Templar, known for hoarding treasures and relics, snatched the Shroud.

Yet, nothing was heard of the Shroud of Turin until 150 years later.

In April, 1349, as the Black Death ravaged Europe, a French knight wrote to Pope Clement VI reporting his intention to build a church at Lirey in France.

The knight named Geoffrey de Charny built the St. Mary of Lirey church to honour God for helping his miraculous escape from the English.

We know that he put the shroud on public exhibition in his church in Lirey in France in 1354.

Large crowds of pilgrims flocked to the church and special souvenir medallions were made in honour of the Shroud.

A single surviving medallion is on display at the Cluny Museum in Paris.

A local bishop was outraged and refusing to believe that the Shroud was genuine, he ordered the exhibition closed. The Shroud was then hidden away for decades.

It passed through many hands, and its ownership was bitterly contested down through the centuries.

We know it was owned by the Savoy family of France by 1453 and they brought it to Chambery.

The shroud was stored in a casket with four locks at Sainte Chapelle in Chambery when a fire broke out in the church on December 4, 1532.

Fire raged around the casket but Canon Philibert Lambert and two Franciscans managed to rescue it.

Melted by the heat, they had to call for the help of a blacksmith to open the grille.

They found that the shroud had survived apart from some scorching and a burn hole caused by a drop of molten silver.

The Poor Clare nuns in Chambery worked from April 16 to May 2, 1534 repairing the shroud. They sewed it onto a backing cloth, and patched the worst of the damage.

Records show that fourteen large triangular patches and eight smaller ones were sewn onto the cloth.

When French troops invaded the Chambery region the following year, the Duke of Savoy, Charles III, fled to Italy with the Shroud.

For the first time ever, the Shroud was exhibited in Turin on May 4, 1535.

The cloth moved around Italy for the next couple of hundred years.

In 1898, an amateur photographer called Secondo Pia was invited to photograph it for the first time.

Secondo was astonished to discover that the Shroud is like a photo negative.

He saw that the negative image is far clearer than the original, revealing wounds that match biblical accounts of the crucifixion.

This negative image startled the world, and the global fascination with the Shroud that began in 1898 continues today.

The study of the relic has even become a scholarly field known as sindonology, from the Greek sindon, meaning linen or linen covering.

Even today Sindonologists come from almost every field of scientific research.

Sindonologists range from staunch believers to atheists and from to those who believe the shroud is a fraud to those who believe it is the burial shroud of Christ.

Despite being a Christian icon of worldwide renown, the Vatican did not gain ownership of the Shroud until the 1980s.

It was Umberto II, a former king of Italy and a member of the House of Savoy which owned the Shroud since 1453, who bequeathed it to Vatican on his death in 1983.

Throughout its history, the Vatican has never confirmed or denied the shroud's authenticity.

Yet, Pope John Paul II spoke about the Shroud and prayed before it at the Turin cathedral on May 24, 1998.

"The Shroud is an image of God's love as well as of human sin," he said.

He added the imprint *"attests to the tremendous human capacity for causing pain and death"* and is *"an icon of the suffering of the innocent in every age."*

Former Pope Benedict XVI said that the shroud's image *"reminds us always"* of Christ's suffering.

Pope Francis has kept to Vatican policy and referred to the shroud as an *"icon"* not a relic.

Despite this, the Shroud is known to Italians as *"La Sindone"* or the Holy Shroud, and it is one of Christianity's greatest objects of veneration.

As one of the prized artefacts of Christianity, it attracts millions of pilgrims to the Cathedral of Saint John the Baptist in Turin.

The Science

The origin and nature of the Shroud of Turin have been sources of debate for decades, and they remain a mystery even today.

In 1978, a team of American scientists called The Shroud of Turin Research Project spent 120 hours studying the Shroud.

They set out to forensically examine the image, discover how it was made, and reveal if it was a fake. They didn't succeed in their aims.

Their report concluded that the creation of the image remains a mystery.

They confirmed that the shroud is not a painting as the image is only a few fibres deep and paint or dye would penetrate further.

The image is a photographic negative and is three-dimensional so it did not come from a brush.

Their analyses found no artificial pigments and they concluded: *"The Shroud image is that of a real human form of a scourged, crucified man. It is not the product of an artist."*

As for what formed the image, the scientists were baffled. They admitted that *"no combination of physical, chemical, biological or medical circumstances"* could explain it.

Radiocarbon Testing

When in 1988, three laboratories in Oxford, Zurich and Arizona radiocarbon dated the Shroud to the Middle Ages, it seemed the debate over the Shroud was over.

Their test results were conclusive. After conducting tests on fibres from the cloth, each confirmed that the fabric dated somewhere between 1260 to 1390.

The results ruled out the possibility of it being a death shroud for Jesus 2,000 years ago.

Overnight, the media dubbed the Shroud a medieval forgery.

Time magazine said the results debunked the link with Christ and The New York Times called it a fraud.

However, it wasn't long before other scientists began to cast doubt on the radiocarbon dating. They suggested that the fire in the 1500s may have altered its carbon content.

Some researchers claimed that the piece tested had actually been a patch added during the medieval repair job.

Newer scientific tests are also contradicting the 1988 results and have dated the cloth to ancient times.

Tests by scientists at the University of Padua in Italy, used the same fibres from the 1988 tests, but disputed the earlier findings.

They repeat the claim that the earlier results were contaminated by fibres used to repair the cloth in the Middle Ages.

Their examination dated the fabric to between 300 BC and 400 AD, which would put it in the era of Christ.

The findings are detailed in a book called The Mystery of the Shroud, by Giulio Fanti, a professor of mechanical and thermal measurement in Padua.

Fanti used infra-red light and spectroscopy - the measurement of radiation intensity - during his 15 years of research for the book.

Blood Testing

Scientific tests proved that the blood stains on the Shroud are real and separate from whatever formed the image of the man on the cloth.

The image of the man does not penetrate the cloth's fibres, only the blood. Scientists say that the blood preceded the imprint of the man.

"Blood first, image second" is a mantra of Shroud researchers.

This supports biblical claims that Jesus was wrapped in the linen days before the resurrection which caused the imprint.

The blood was identified as Type AB which is also the same blood type contained in the relics of the Eucharistic Miracle of Lanciano.

Researchers have also recently released a report suggesting that the blood on the Shroud is from a torture victim.

Institute of Crystallography researcher, Elvio Carlino, said the blood is from a person undergoing "great suffering".

He discovered it contains "nanoparticles" of blood which are not found in a healthy person and says constituents in the blood only occur in humans who have suffered severe trauma.

"A scenario of violence is recorded in the funeral fabric," he wrote in the scientific article.

Professor Giulio Fanti, another author of the research, said: *"The presence of these biological nanoparticles found during our experiments point to a violent death for the man wrapped in the Turin Shroud."*

Confirming the authenticity of the Shroud is the fact its blood stains are linked to another holy relic from the time when Jesus walked the earth.

Experts have claimed another ancient cloth linked to Jesus replicates the same blood flows and blood type as the Shroud.

The cloth called the Sudarium of Oviedo resides in the Cathedral of Oviedo, in Spain.

Believers claim it was placed over the head of Jesus when his followers managed to lower him from the cross.

According to the Gospels, the Apostles discovered a discarded head cloth as well as the shroud in Christ's empty tomb.

The Gospel of John 20:7 noted that they found *"the face cloth, which had been on Jesus' head, not lying with the linen cloths but folded up in a place by itself."*

While the Sudarium does not contain a facial image, it contains blood of the type AB found on the Shroud.

Moreover, the patterns of blood flow on the Sudarium are consistent with those of a crucified man.

American Sudarium expert, Janice Bennett, says there are 20 points of correlation between the Shroud and the relic in Spain.

Pollen Testing

Tests on the Shroud have also found imprints of flowers and traces of pollen that could only have come from the Holy Land.

Studies suggest that bunches or bouquets of flowers and floral materials were placed on the Shroud. They left pollen grains and imprints of plants and flowers on the linen cloth.

Both the pollen, which has been dated to the first century, and the imprints match flowers found in the vicinity of Jerusalem.

The Council for Study of the Turin Shroud from Duke University noted: *"While there are images of hundreds of flowers on the Shroud, many are vague or incomplete. We feel we have identified, tentatively but with reasonable certainty, twenty-eight plants whose images are sufficiently clear ... All twenty-eight grow in Israel."*

Crucifixion Testing

Many see it as an unlikely coincidence that the wounds of the man on the Shroud match the exact biblical description of Jesus's crucifixion.

From piercings on his head from the 'crown of thorns' to the piercing in his side, the man on the Shroud reflects all the injuries inflicted on Jesus.

The only details that originally didn't appear to match were the appearance of nail wounds on the man's wrists, rather than his palms.

All religious art depicting the crucifixion of Jesus showed the nail in the palms of the hand.

However, sindonologist Dr. Pierre Barbet, tested crucifixion techniques on cadavers donated to science.

He discovered, that driving nails through 'Destot's Space', between the tendons at the wrist, was necessary to support the weight of crucified men.

Many believe that this historically accurate detail, which was unknown in the middle ages, is a further sign that the Shroud is unlikely to be a forgery from that era.

Radiation Testing

First among the mysteries of the Shroud is how the man's image was made. Some say the imprint could be described as an intricate singe marking on the linen.

Yet, every scientific attempt to replicate the Shroud in a lab has failed.

One of the more bizarre features of the Shroud is the X-ray details of the man's teeth and fingers. Nothing existed in medieval or ancient times that could produce X-rays like this.

In 1989, physicist Thomas Phillips speculated that a large burst of radiation emitted during the resurrection created the image on the Shroud.

But scientists have tried and failed using ultraviolet radiation to make the image on the Shroud.

In a 2015 article for National Geographic, Italian physicist Paolo Di Lazzaro admitted they are no closer to understanding how the image was made.

"(The Shroud's) precise hue is highly unusual, and the colour's penetration into the fabric is extremely thin, less than ... one-thirtieth the diameter of an individual fibre in a single 200-fibre linen thread," he claimed.

Di Lazzaro and colleagues experimented for five years with lasers to replicate the image on linen.

Using short bursts of ultraviolet light, they came close to replicating the image's distinctive colour.

But they admitted that they could not reproduce a whole human figure.

Di Lazzaro claimed that the ultraviolet light needed to reproduce the image *"exceeds the maximum power released by all ultraviolet light sources available today."*

A Reflection on the Shroud of Turin

There will always be Doubting Thomases in this world, so there will always be those who question the Shroud of Turin.

Scientists, with all their vast modern technology, have tried and failed to reproduce the image on the Shroud.

Yet, some people are still determined to believe that forgers in medieval times managed to do it.

Even Jesus found it very hard to make a Doubting Thomas believe.

The Apostle Thomas only believed that Jesus rose from the dead when Our Lord appeared in front of him and let him feel his wounds.

Jesus said, *"Blessed [are] they that have not seen, and [yet] have believed."*

Believers don't need the Shroud of Turin to be authenticated to believe in the resurrection of Jesus.

Yet rational scientific evidence points towards the Shroud being a living testimony of the death and resurrection of Christ.

As such, the Shroud is the perfect example of the fusion of faith and science.

Science is now corroborating our faith and our belief in the eyewitness accounts we read in the Bible.

And science is helping make it even more apparent that the Shroud is an authentic sign of God in the world.

In fact, if there is a Doubting Thomas who needed evidence of the existence of God, the Shroud of Turin could be it.

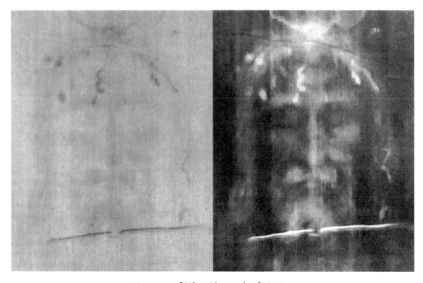

Image of The Shroud of Turin

Image of The Shroud of Turin

PART THREE

GOD'S REVELATION IN THE WORLD

Great are the works of the Lord;
they are pondered by all who delight in them.
Glorious and majestic are his deeds,
and his righteousness endures forever.
He has caused his wonders to be remembered;

Psalm 111:2-4

God's Revelation in the World

Introduction

We're surrounded by evidence of God's hand in this spectacular world, but many fail to recognise it.

There are miracle claims around the world that defy scientific scrutiny and mounting evidence from scientists that point towards a divine creator.

Yet, many choose to dismiss God saying that science has proved our highly-organised universe and this beautiful earth came about by mere chance.

And there's a common perception in the modern world that God is going out of fashion and religion is on the wane.

It's true that too many people spend far more of their time gazing into their screens than looking into their souls.

No one has breathing space for prayer between checking their email, Facebook and Instagram.

And there's a growing indifference to faith among many, especially in the Western world.

"I'm more spiritual than religious," you'll hear people say.

In other words, they're saying: *"I'll take the nice 'spiritual' label but hold the mass, the sacrifice, the prayer or any effort at all to know God."*

There are younger generations with short attention spans and a worldview that doesn't include a divine being.

They see the Bible as a dusty two-thousand-year-old parchment which doesn't apply to their lives. Or they see religious practice as a quaint notion for older people.

There's groupthink that's never challenged with phrases like: *"no one believes in God anymore"* and *"sure, science has proved there's no God."*

And it's tough for even the committed Christian to hear God in the modern world with all the distractions around.

Everything is fast-paced and furious, and there's so much busyness that the task of living a God-centred life is a challenging one.

Then faith is continuously tested with a growing perception that God and religion are on the way out. Tradition, ritual, reflection and prayer are considered old-fashioned and irrelevant.

Belief is disparaged with quips from eminent names like the late Stephen Hawking who said heaven is *"a fairy story for people afraid of the dark."*

It's fair to say that the sacred is under attack from the rising tide of the secular, but there's no evidence that it's winning that battle.

In fact, in Part 3 of this book, I'm looking at how the numbers of believers in the world are actually on the rise and far exceed the unbelievers.

And contrary to popular belief, scientific research is not disproving God. Instead, it's making the most significant argument there is for God's revelation in the world.

It's as if in the face of the rising tide of secularism, that God is revealing Himself through modern science.

At a time when believers needs more reassurance than ever, God has surrounded us with even more evidence of his existence.

Can 5.8 Billion People Be Wrong?

"Then the Lord took Abram outside and said to him,
"Look up into the sky and count the stars if you can.
That's how many descendants you will have!"
Genesis 15:5

God has been revealing himself to the world since the dawn of time.

As a result evidence of religious worship on Earth goes back thousands of years.

Religious rites such as burials with grave goods which are 100,000 years old have been found in Israel.

Cave paintings in Chauvet in France show forms of worship taking place among humans 32,000 years ago.

The oldest known megalithic temple that survives today is Gobekli Tepe in Turkey which was built around 10,000 BC.

So, since humankind has existed, man has wondered about the mysteries of the universe and believed in a divine being or beings who created it.

No doubt they saw evidence of god in the magnificence of the milky way. And they saw angry gods in natural phenomenon like thunder, eclipses and earthquakes.

Major world religions began emerging about 3000BC with the invention of writing.

The 'Big 5' consisting of Christianity, Hinduism, Islam, Judaism and Buddhism have grown in dominance over the last 2,000 years.

The influence of religion was pervasive across politics, society and economics in Europe for more than a thousand years.

This lessened with the age of enlightenment as science began to explain away the magical thinking of our ancestors.

We gradually moved away from the traditional structures, dogma and doctrines of the major Christian religions.

Until fifty years ago, when Time magazine sounded the death toll for religion with the cover page title, 'Is God Dead?'

The issue caused outrage and the publishers were accused of blasphemy when it was published in 1966.

Even the singer Bob Dylan addressed the furore, albeit with mock horror: *"If you were God, how would you like to see that written about yourself?"*

In fact, many people would be forgiven for thinking ever since that religion is on the wane all over the world.

We hear endless reports of the decline in mass attendance and the drop in vocations.

We hear how the clerical child sex abuse scandals have cast a shadow over the Catholic church worldwide.

With so much negativity surrounding religion, is it any wonder that some are drifting away from their Christian upbringing?

Christianity in the Western world could be doing better, that's for sure.

And the Church has to shoulder some of the blame for the shameful scandals of its past.

It could do more to proclaim the good news of our loving and all-powerful creator in a more energetic way.

For example, I'm always mindful too that in Ireland, priests are mostly preaching to the choir.

With priests being scarce on the ground, it's practical to prioritise and focus our attention on the faithful.

Time and resources are scarce, and we are in our comfort zone tending to the faithful. But the Church has to find ways of reach out beyond our comfort zone.

We need to spread out and engage with younger people particularly.

It's easy to see how younger generations see less need for a God when a credit card seems to meet all their needs.

It's easier too to binge-watch Godless on Netflix rather than engage in a more challenging exploration of faith and spirituality.

With eyes trained on handheld devices and an obsession with the digital world, it's harder to grab this generation's attention.

The top Google search which includes the word "God" is "God of War," the action adventure video game for example.

For many young people God has become an old-fashioned concept that belongs to previous generations.

Religion is regarded as irrational and irrelevant as the mysteries of the universe are unlocked by science.

So instead young people are blindly following a cosy social consensus that excludes the possibility of a divine creator.

The young are in their comfort zone in front of Netflix and we in the Church are in our comfort zone with an ageing cohort of believers.

We need to change to reach this generation and young people need to explore beyond peer groupthink.

Everyone has to see that the argument *"sure no one believes in God anymore"* is a mistaken one.

Because, to borrow a phrase, the rumours of God's death are greatly exaggerated.

Even in this era where we talk of global secularisation, the numbers of believers in the world still vastly out numbers the non-believers.

And the common assumption that religion is in decline is also wrong.

Research that we detail shows that there are 5.8 billion believers in this world and their numbers are growing at a rapid pace.

All the evidence and polls consistently show that belief in God is very much alive and well and is universal.

Even amid all the distractions of the modern world, it seems people crave the inclusivity, the connectedness and caring guidance of God's word in their lives.

Far from being an outdated notion, religion can be a force that transforms our troubled times.

The question that Time magazine posed all those years ago was not *'Is God Dead?'* but *'Is God Relevant in the Modern Era'*?

But *'Is God Relevant?'* wouldn't have sold as many copies as the provocative *'Is God Dead?'*

If the vast majority on the planet are claiming to have a relationship with religion, the answer must be that God is very much relevant and alive.

Ireland: The Land Of Saints And Secularists?

Around 400AD, there was a Roman teenager, who may or may not have been called Maewyn Succat. Let's call him that anyway for now.

He lived in relative comfort in a settlement at Bonavem Taberniae, which was possibly in the modern town of Kilpatrick, in Scotland.

It could also have been Cumbria in England. Or even in northern France.

We do know that the teenager's parents, Calphurnius and Conchessa were from an eminent and wealthy Roman family of clerics.

His father was a deacon, his mother, Conchessa was a Gaul from modern day France. She was also either a sister or a niece of St. Martin of Tours.

Maewyn, like many teenagers today, had no interest in religion at all.

Years later, he wrote in his *Confessio* that he *'blush and fear exceedingly'* when he thought back to his lack of knowledge and education in religion.

When he was around 16-years old, pirates raided his father's estate.

Before he knew it, he and many of his father's workers were taken prisoner and bundled on board the pirate ship.

They were brought as slaves to a region called Dál Riada which was around present day County Antrim.

The boy, who would come to be known as Saint Patrick, was put to work in the bitter cold, driving rain and barren hills keeping herds of sheep, goats and cattle.

Patrick's master, Milchu, was a pagan and high priest of Druidism which held sway over the Irish population.

While isolated in the hills of Ireland, Patrick turned to God and regarded his enslavement as a test of his faith.

By the time he escaped after six years of captivity, he was deeply devoted to Christianity.

He studied for the priesthood in France and was ordained a deacon by the Bishop of Auxerre around 418 A.D.

In 432 A.D. he was ordained a bishop and Pope Celestine gave him the name Patrick. The name Patrick or in its original form, Patricius, derives from the Latin term for "father figure".

No one would have blamed Patrick if he never came back here again, but in a vision he saw the pagans of Ireland extending their hands to him.

Despite the terrible hospitality shown to him the last time he'd visited, he returned to convert the Irish to Christianity.

Patrick wasn't the first missionary to arrive in Ireland.

The earliest began to arrive just as the Roman Empire collapsed during the fourth and fifth centuries.

As Europe began disintegrating into the Dark Ages, a little beacon of light and hope started flickering on this island.

Far removed from the social decay of the continent, Ireland became a haven for Christian missionaries.

It was only with the arrival of Saint Patrick in the first half of the fifth century, that Christianity firmly took hold.

Ireland's renown as the Land of Saints and Scholars began.

The island basked in a warm celestial glow for many hundreds of years and was regarded as one of the most religious countries on earth.

In the Middle Ages, when the Christian faith began to collapse across Western Europe, Ireland started exporting many of these saints and scholars back again.

It was Irish missionaries who reignited the flame of faith all over the continent and beyond.

For a hundred years before Columbanus began his great missions in Europe, there were Irish pilgrims and bishops already in Gaul and Italy.

Other Irish missionaries like Columcille spread the faith across Scotland and England.

He was so successful that by 662, there was only one bishop in the whole of England who wasn't ordained in Ireland. Even this bishop, a Frenchman, had been trained for many years in Ireland.

The Catholic faith here faced its greatest threat with the introduction of the Penal Laws in Ireland in the 16th and 17th centuries.

The now totally Protestant parliaments in Ireland and Britain imposed fines and imprisonment for Catholic worship and a penalty of death to priests who practised mass.

The first of the Penal Laws was passed in 1697 and ordered almost all bishops, priests, monks and nuns to leave the country. As a result hundreds of clergy were transported to France.

There were penalties for Catholic bishops and priests who remained in Ireland without permission.

Substantial rewards of £20.00 (around €6,000 in modern currency) were offered for information leading to the capture of a priest, and £50.00 (€15,000) for a bishop. This led to the arrival of the dreaded "priest hunters" or the bounty hunters of the era.

Some priests wore lay clothes, became employed as farm labourers, and ministered in secret to their people.

On many occasions Mass was offered in the open air with a flat rock or a stone taken from a church ruin serving as an altar. Mass services were carried out secretly and parishioners were alerted to the services by word of mouth.

The custom of placing a lighted candle on the window at Christmas is also said to come from the days of the Penal Laws.

Candles were lit in windows as a signal to the wandering priests of the time that it was a safe house and that the family wanted to receive the sacraments.

Despite centuries of oppression and persecution, the population clung to their religion and the country remained staunchly Catholic by the beginning of the 19th century.

However, there were few priests, schools or church buildings.

The Church remained poor and disorganised until the appointment of Paul Cullen as Archbishop of Dublin in the 1850s.

Cullen, who Ireland's first Cardinal, he sought *'to rescue this Catholic country from the . . . religious inferiority in which it now lies.'*

He set about reforming the Irish Church and reinforcing the authority of Rome. He established almost 40 religious foundations, schools, hospitals and 20 new churches as well as a huge increase in the number of clergy, nuns and brothers.

He turned Catholicism into a powerful political and social entity across Ireland. The Church continued to wield huge sway here right up to the late 20th Century.

However, its influence on Irish society begin to wane in the 60s, as it did all over the Western World.

Since then, statistical evidence, and even the evidence of our own eyes, can leave us in no doubt that mass attendance is dropping.

The most recent census in 2016 shows 10 per cent or 468,421 people declared they had no religion.

The media talked of a *'looming crisis'* for the Church.

There was even a headline reading: "*Irish Catholicism is Dying - No New Priests and Falling Mass Attendance.*"

With so much anecdotal evidence and so many similar reports in the media, it would seem that believers are an endangered species in Ireland.

Yes, it's true that census data from 2016 indicates that 10 per cent now identify themselves as non-believers in Ireland.

But the good news is that it means a massive 90 per cent of the Irish population are believers.

A huge majority of those believers, 78 per cent, are Catholics according to the census.

So, it's a stretch to claim that the Church in Ireland is *'in crisis'* or *'is dying'* or is being replaced by secularism.

We also have plenty of evidence that young adults in Ireland are still practising their faith in great numbers.

According to the results of the latest European Social Survey, young people here remain among the most religious in Europe.

The survey found that 54 per cent of young adults aged between 16-29 in Ireland claim Catholic affiliation.

Saint Patrick himself, who wasn't a great believer in his own youth, would find those figures encouraging.

But being the great missionary, Patrick was, he'd still encourage us to get out there and reach out to those not in the fold.

Because Jesus is never happy until all the flock is safe in His fold and we shouldn't be either.

He wants to reach out and find those who are not engaging with God.

Jesus says: *"I have other sheep that are not in this sheepfold. I must bring them also. They too will listen to my voice and there will be one fold and one shepherd."* John 10.16

The Church has faced many crises from Viking raids to Penal Laws and persecution to the rise of secularism and the abuse scandals in religious institutions.

Yet despite all the trials and tribulations that have threatened the Church over the last 1,500 years, the good news is that the faith of our fathers continues to survive and thrive in Ireland.

A Whole Wide World Of God

How does God fare outside of Ireland in an era when secularism is growing on a global scale?

The impact of the modern world on religion worldwide may be vastly overstated here too.

God isn't going anywhere if you look at the results of some of the most recent global research.

The Pew Research Centre in America, a nonpartisan fact tank, compiled a study on the global religious landscape in 2012.

According to their figures, more than eight-in-ten people in the world identify with a religious group.

They gleaned information about billions of people from around the world using 2,500 censuses to reach their results.

Their research revealed that there are 5.8 billion in the world are religiously affiliated.

That number represents 84% of the 2010 world population of almost 7 billion people.

These figures are largely replicated in most other surveys.

Adherents.com, which collates religious demographics worldwide, concurs that 84% of the world population have religious beliefs.

The Association of Religious Data Archives estimated in 2010 that 88% of the world population have religious beliefs.

So, it appears that 5.8 billion out of 7 billion identify as having religious affiliation.

Can that many people be wrong?

According to the Encyclopaedia Britannica, 2% of the world's population self-identify as atheists.

Another 2004 survey by the CIA in the World Factbook estimates about 2.4% are atheists.

Atheist numbers are also expected to grow smaller according to Pew because of the low birth rate recorded in the demographic.

Yet, the numbers of religious people are expected to expand from 5.8 billion to 8.1 billion by 2050.

So, is God relevant anymore?

All the evidence suggests that the vast majority of human beings, everywhere in the world, at all times, are believers in some version of religion.

Human beings need to believe that they are a part of something bigger. Many inherently know that the material world will never satisfy them and they crave something more.

As long as they continue to do so, God remains very relevant and central to the lives of a lot of people everywhere on the globe.

One World, Many Faiths, One God

According to some estimates, there may be 10,000 different religions in the world.

There are about 40 major divisions in Christianity alone and thousands of Christian denominations.

The 'Big Five' are Christianity, Islam, Hinduism, Buddhism and Judaism.

But other large groupings of faiths include Baha'i, Confucianism, Jainism, Shinto, Sikhism, Taoism, and Zoroastrianism.

With so many religions out there, there would appear to be a lot of people out there following a lot of different Gods.

People searching for the truth often wonder, which religion is the right one?

Which one is the true God?

The fact is that most people know that the truth has many faces and versions.

Even people who witness the same event will see the event differently.

If someone relates a story, no two people listening will repeat it the same way.

People may see and hear the exact same occurrence, but each will see and hear different aspects.

They can come away with different meanings.

Just as people interpret the truth differently, they hear God's voice in different ways.

For Christians, the teachings of Jesus is the true voice of God. Jesus is God, and we live by the word of the Bible.

Meanwhile, Jews see their God in the words of the Torah.

Muslims believe Jesus is a prophet and instead follow the word of Allah, and they live by the instructions of the Quran.

But, all of these faiths and indeed most major religions around the world spread the same message: Love God, love your brothers and sisters as yourself, and do good in the world.

And proclaiming that you're a Christian, or a Muslim or a Hindu is not enough either.

You can go to mass, the mosque or the temple every day, but all faiths demand that their followers also show their love for God by their actions.

According to Jesus: *"Not everyone who says to me, "Lord, Lord," will enter the kingdom of heaven, but only those who do the will of my Father who is in heaven.* (Matthew 7:21)

So many religions in the world have more in common with each other than they have differences.

In fact, many people are not aware that Christians share a common religious heritage with Islam and Judaism.

Together Christians, Muslims and Jews form by far the biggest religious grouping in the world.

Abrahamism

More than 3.8 billion believers around the world belong to the Abrahamic religions.

This is the biggest belief system in the world combining 2.2 billion Christians of which 1.15 billion people are Catholic.

Our Abrahamic brothers include 1.6 billion Muslims and 14 million Jews.

All three religions trace their origins to the prophet Abraham and the ancient Israelites.

Abraham was the first person to teach that there is only one God.

The God who spoke to Abraham is now the same God of all Christians, Muslims and Jews.

Abraham is an important foundation stone in all three faiths.

He is referred to in the five-times daily prayers of Muslims.

Meanwhile, Jewish scripture in the Torah, says Abraham received a covenant from God which makes them the chosen people.

Abraham is a major figure for Christians in the Bible. Christians first learn about Abraham in Genesis, the first book of sacred scripture in the Old Testament.

The Old Testament even explains the earliest divisions in the Abrahamic faiths.

Genesis tells us after the flood destroyed the world 6,000 years ago, Noah and his descendants repopulate the earth.

Generations later, the people once again turn away from God and start to build the Tower of Babel to allow them to reach heaven.

God scatters Noah's descendants to the four corners of the world all speaking in different languages.

He offers a covenant to Abraham that in return for his faithfulness, he will make his descendants as numerous as the stars of the sky.

Having descendants appears unlikely as Abraham's wife Sarah remains barren well into old age.

So Sarah and Abraham arrange for him to have a son with an Egyptian slave girl called Hagar.

He calls his first-born son Ishmael.

Some years later Sarah bears him a son, as God promised, and they call him Isaac.

Then tensions arise between Sarah and Hagar over inheritance rights and Abraham sends Hagar and Ishmael away into the desert.

The first split in the Abrahamic religions comes as the two sons of Abraham are sent their separate ways.

The second son Isaac grows up to become the father of the Jewish nation.

Isaac's descendants include the great King David who rules the Jewish nation.

A thousand years later another great Jewish descendant, Jesus, is born.

After Jesus dies, there is another split in the Abrahamic faith system.

When the Jews reject Jesus Christ as the Messiah, the followers of Christ, which means 'anointed one' in Greek, became known as Christians.

In the 2,000 years since, Christians have become the most populous religion in the world.

Meanwhile, what happened to Abraham's first son Ishmael?

He went off into the desert, and he and his many descendants founded the Arab nation.

Then six hundred years after Jesus lived on earth, a descendant of Ishmael called Muhammad claimed he had visions from God.

He proclaimed that the descendants of Ishmael in the nation of Islam were the true inheritors of God's covenant with Abraham, not the Jewish nation.

Islam was born and Muslims are now the second most populous religion in the world.

Ishmael and his mother Hagar are said to be buried next to the Kaaba in Mecca.

Out of a world population of 7 billion approximately, more than 3.8 billion are Abrahamic using figures from the 2012 survey by the Pew in America.

Christianity, Islam and Judaism in all their forms still thrive in modern times.

And God kept his Old Testament promise to Abraham to make his descendants as numerous as the stars of the sky - as the Abrahamic faiths now represent over half of the entire world's population.

God Is Good For Your Health

It's a good thing that the numbers of believers are thriving and rising - because there's a link between good mental health and religion.

Experts have proven countries with higher levels of non-believers also have a higher suicide rate.

The American Journal of Psychiatry published a report in 2004 that confirmed previous studies showing a link between religion and suicide.

Their study of depressed patients confirmed that 'religiously unaffiliated' subjects had significantly more lifetime suicide attempts.

The same patients also had more close relatives who committed suicide.

Researchers found that subjects with no religion saw less reasons for living and had fewer moral objections to suicide.

They discovered that they showed more impulsivity, aggression, and past substance use disorder.

They concluded that people with religion have greater protective factors against suicide.

They have more moral objections to suicide and have lower aggression levels which leads to fewer attempts.

It's Never Too Late

As I finish writing this section, I read with interest that a former head of State in Australia has renounced atheism and converted to Catholicism - after being inspired by an Irish nun.

Australia's former governor-general, Bill Hayden, a life-long atheist, has been baptised at the age of 85.

After living as a non-believer most of his adult life, the former politician revealed he has joined the Catholic Church.

One of Australia's iconic Labour leaders, he turned to the Church in response to the "gnawing pain in my heart and soul about the meaning of life."

I was particularly interested to see he was inspired after witnessing the good life and works of Christians especially Sister of Mercy, Angela Mary Doyle.

Sister Angela, who is 93-years-old and travelled from Ireland to Australia in 1948, is famous for her work with the poor in Brisbane.

Hayden said he and his wife, Dallas, went to visit the Sister in a hospital in Brisbane and "felt embraced and loved by her Christian example."

"*Dallas, our daughter Ingrid and I recently visited Sister Angela Mary in the Mater Hospital where she was a patient,*" he recalled. "*The next morning, I woke with the strong sense that I had been in the presence of a holy woman. So, after dwelling on these things I found my way back to the core of those beliefs - the Church.*"

Hayden admitted he began reflecting on his life following a stroke in 2014. He was further inspired by witnessing many selfless acts of compassion by Christians during his lifetime.

"*This took too long, and now I am going to be devoted,*" he said. "*From this day forward, I'm going to vouch for God.*"

Following his stroke in 2014, the political leader said he discovered "*more to life than just me.*"

He said: "*I had to make a dedication of myself for the good of others, before God. I felt that strongly.*"

After all these years, he felt he could no longer maintain his atheist beliefs.

"*Christianity is about love for your fellow humans, forgiveness, compassion and helpful support,*" he said. "*These characteristics are founded on the teachings of Christ and driven by faith in an external power. I can no longer accept that human existence is self-sufficient and isolated.*"

This story reminds me of that American Redemptorist priest that lectured us in the Beda. He pleaded with us to learn to live the Seven Virtues. If we live the Virtues, he promised us that we would inspire people around us to turn to God as Sister Angela clearly does.

My wife Liz lived the virtues, especially the virtues of love, hope and faith, and she even inspired me, a slow learner, to want to know God.

It's good to know that there are even slower learners who wait until they're 85 to let God into their lives. It just shows that it's never too late for any of us!

Is Science Proving the Existence of God?

"Of course, every house is constructed by someone,
but he that constructed all things is God."
Hebrews 3:4.

God's presence will always be felt through worship and the sacraments, but He also manifests himself throughout every aspect of life, nature and the cosmos.

Scientists believe that our universe began with a giant explosion of energy and light.

The universe *"was a hundred thousand million degrees Centigrade…and the universe was filled with light,"* [1] says Nobel laureate in physics, Steven Weinberg.

The description almost echoes the Biblical one: *"And God said, 'Let there be light: and there was light.'"* Genesis 1:3

News that the world began in a vast ball of cosmic combustion was all some people need to remove God from creation.

They have this idea that every wonder of the natural world has a scientific explanation and claims of scripture like 'God made the world in seven days' are ridiculous.

"There's no such thing as God; Science has proved it all started with the big bang," is a common argument.

And many people are still mistakenly cocooned in this cosy consensus that God has been made obsolete thanks to science.

---

[1] Steven Weinberg; The First Three Minutes: A Modern View of the Origin of the Universe; 1977

They say the need for man to worship a divine creator is disappearing as science uncovers the mysteries of the universe.

We know that many young adults say that one of the reasons they have left the Church is because they see a disconnect between science and religion.

Two American studies[2] into young people leaving the faith revealed some of the typical reasons for loss of belief included the following sentiments:

"Because I grew up realised it was a story like Santa or the Easter Bunny."

"Catholic beliefs aren't based on fact. Everything is hearsay from back before anything could be documented, so nothing can be disproved, but it certainly shouldn't be taken seriously."

"It no longer fits into what I understand of the universe."

"I realised that religion is in complete contradiction with the rational and scientific world, and to continue to subscribe to a religion would be hypocritical."

This *"science-has-proved-that-there-is-no-God"* notion seems to be an accepted fact among people.

It's a statement that's rarely contradicted, questioned or investigated.

Yet the truth is that science, instead of disproving God, is increasingly making the argument for a Divine Creator.

As science progresses and unravels some of the mysteries of the world, more and more experts are baffled by the revelations.

The complexities of the universe that have been uncovered and unravelled by science have astounded some of the most eminent boffins on earth.

The real truth is that some of the greatest scientists in the world are now recognising the finger-prints of intelligent design in the universe.

---

[2]   Centre for Applied Research in the Apostolate in America (CARA)

And there should be no disconnect between science and faith. In fact, the more that people learn about science, the more it should strengthen their faith.

Everything points to a Divine Creator who not only designed a complex universe but still sustains it today.

The Sacred Vs the Scientific

There's no doubt that for the past 500 years, religion and science have had a rocky relationship.

Many have argued down through the centuries that scientific enquiry is incompatible with religious belief.

Yet, it's only a few zealots in both the fields of religion and science that can be blamed for this clash.

The so-called 'father of science' Galileo Galilei was tried for heresy in 1633 for believing that the sun, rather than the earth, was the centre of the solar system.

"I do not feel obliged to believe that the same God who has endowed us with senses, reason and intellect has intended up to forego their use," argued Galileo reasonably.

But as knowledge grew, many scientists believed they were God-like beings, peeling away the mysteries of the world.

They believed God was no longer in the equation.

The battle between science and religion began in earnest with the publication of Charles Darwin's The Origin of the Species.

The whole theory of evolution appeared to clash with the teachings of the church.

The Bible tells us on the fourth and fifth days of creation that God *"created great whales, and every living creature that moveth"* and *"made the beast of the earth"*.

Scientists scoffed that this was crackpot, supernatural nonsense. They said rational thinking and observational evidence proved that life on earth evolved.

Dynamic biology created life, not God.

The notion of a divine creator making the world was pooh-poohed, and religion was dismissed as primitive superstition or magical thinking.

Even back then, however, many Christians saw evolution and creation as compatible bedfellows.

They were open to the idea that evolution was another instrument of God's design.

Darwin, himself, in several editions of The Origin of the Species, referred to *"the Creator."*

Still, most scientific thinkers believed that there was a gulf between creation-evolution theories that could not be breached.

They scoffed at the notion of a Divine Creator or even a creative intelligence.

Mass, space and energy always existed, so our universe never had a beginning they said. The world was a self-sufficient mechanical and changeless system.

They were adamant that evolution and natural selection designed life on Earth, not God.

The Big Bang

Back in the nineteenth century, astronomers believed that our own Milky Way was the entire universe.

Today, thanks to advances in space exploration we know there are trillions of stars in one hundred billion galaxies that are expanding all the time.

However, astronomers using limited telescopes in the early 20th century, could not detect the expansion of the universe.

They assumed that the world was static and never had a beginning.

Yet even then, the evidence for a universe without a beginning was not adding up.

Albert Einstein's equations told him that the universe could not stay static. It had to either expand or contract.

He ignored what his mathematics was telling him. He later reputedly called it *"the biggest blunder of my life."*

Einstein and most scientists insisted that the universe was *"simply there"* with no beginning or end.

However, it took a Catholic priest from Belgium to send the scientific world into a tailspin.

His theory of the origins of the world in the 1920s revolutionised thinking on the origins of the universe.

Fr George Lemaitre, an astronomer and professor of physics, is now feted as the father of the Big Bang theory.

Lemaitre believed the world started as a fireball many billions of years ago.

He was the first to introduce the idea that the universe started with a singularity in his 'hypothesis of the primaeval atom'.

He believed that the world could be traced to this single point and that the universe was expanding and cooling ever since.

His work moved science on from a point where the world could no longer be seen as a self-sufficient, mechanical and changeless system.

Instead, the world had a beginning, and therefore an end. Suddenly the universe was as vulnerable and precarious as that of human beings.

He presented his new ideas to many sceptical scientists, including Einstein.

Many thought his work was far-fetched.

Years later, his biggest detractor, Fred Hoyle, a professor at Cambridge University, scornfully referred to Lemaitre's work as the 'big bang' theory.

However, Edwin Hubble and others confirmed Lemaitre's hypothesis with mathematics.

Lemaitre's theories were widely accepted by those working in the field of physics and astronomy within a few years.

Albert Einstein is eventually said to have described Lemaitre's work as: *"the most beautiful and satisfactory explanation of creation to which I have ever listened."*

It is important to state that no scientist of repute, including Einstein, has ever claimed to have discovered anything that disproves the existence of God.

In fact, acclaimed theoretical physicist Richard Feynman, while speaking at the California Institute of Technology in the 1950s, said he did not believe that that science will ever disprove the existence of God.

"I think that is impossible," he said. *"And if it is impossible, is not a belief in science and in a God - an ordinary God of religion- a consistent possibility?"*

Fr. Lemaitre's theories that the earth had a beginning were conclusively proved by the Cosmic Background Explorer (COBE) mission in 1992.

Changing our understanding of the early cosmos, COBE finally confirmed the Big Bang theory of the origin of the universe.

Even the Nobel prize-winning scientist, George Smoot, who ran the COBE experiment, saw parallels between the big bang and the Bible.

"There is no doubt that a parallel exists between the big bang as an event and the Christian notion of creation from nothing," he wrote.[3]

---

[3] George Smoot; Wrinkles in Time; 1993

Astrophysicist Robert Jastrow says *"the Universe flashed into being and we cannot find out what caused that to happen."*[4]

He even compared the event to the account in Genesis 1:1 of the origins of the world:

"Now we see how the astronomical evidence leads to a biblical view of the origin of the world," he wrote. [5]

More recently Amir Aczel, a science lecturer in America, noted how the Big Bang dove-tails with many ancient scriptures on the origins of the universe.

"Traditions of Chinese, Indian, pre-Colombian, and African cultures, as well as the biblical book of Genesis, all describe... a distinct beginning to the universe, whether it's the "creation in six days" of Genesis or the "Cosmic Egg" of the ancient Indian text the Rig Veda," he wrote.[6]

He added: *"This is an interesting example of scientists being dead wrong (for a time) and primitive ancient observers having an essentially correct intuition about nature."*

Perfect World Design

A century later and scientists are no closer to disproving the existence of God.

As progress continues, the unfolding mysteries of the universe leave them with more questions than answers.

Cosmologists, who study the universe's origin, claim the intricacies of the world are baffling. They can't understand how a random cosmic explosion could bring about life unless it was engineered to do so.

---

[4]   Robert Jastrow; Message from Professor Robert Jastrow; LeaderU.com; 2002
[5]   Robert Jastrow; God and the Astronomers; 2001
[6]   Amir Aczel; Einstein's Lost Theory Describes a Universe Without a Big Bang; Discover Magazine; 2014

For life to begin, gravity and the other forces of nature needed to be just right.

We now know if the expansion rate in the universe been slightly weaker, the "big bang" would have ended in a "big crunch". Gravity would have pulled all matter back to its original point.

The late physicist and cosmologist Stephen Hawking wrote:

"If the rate of expansion one second after the big bang had been smaller by even one part in a hundred thousand million million, the universe would have re-collapsed before it ever reached its present size." [7]

If the expansion rate was slightly larger, the planets and solar systems would not exist.

More and more frequently we hear words like *"design" "super-intellect,"* and *"creator"* in the lexicon of the scientific world.

And more and more scientists admit that with every stride in progress we make, there is more evidence pointing towards intelligent design.

In fact, the more that we learn about the complexity of the universe, the more scientists are astonished by the odds of human existence at all.

The Wall Street Journal's 2014 article *"Science Increasingly Makes the Case for God,"* has become the most popular online article in the paper's history.

Author Eric Metaxas explained that back in the 1960s, experts believed that an infinite number of planets were capable of supporting life.

Scientists estimated there were one septillion planets - 1 followed by 24 zeros - in the universe capable of having life forms.

The requirements for life were the right kind of star, and a planet the right distance from that star according to the experts.

---

[7]   Stephen Hawking; A Brief History of Time; 1996

By the 1990s, it became clear that there were far more factors necessary for life. The right kind of star and a planet the right distance from that star was not going to be enough.

If Earth was smaller, its gravity wouldn't be enough to hold a thin layer of oxygen extending 50 miles above the earth's surface. If it was larger, the atmosphere would be like Jupiter, full of hydrogen.[8]

The Earth is also the perfect distance from the sun. Any closer and we'd burn up, and any colder and the earth would be a ball of ice.

It also spins on its axis as it hurtles around the sun at a speed of 67,000mph ensuring all the surface of the earth to warm and cool every 24-hours.

"The odds turned against any planet in the universe supporting life, including this one," reported Metaxas in the Wall Street Journal.

Defying the Laws of Probability

Metaxas reported that there are now more than 200 known parameters necessary for a planet to support life.

All of them must be met perfectly, or the whole thing falls apart.

He gives an example of one of the parameters for life on earth:

"Without a massive planet like Jupiter nearby, whose gravity will draw away asteroids, a thousand times as many would hit Earth's surface."

It seems the odds of any life in the universe after a random explosion are so minuscule that the fact we exist at all is simply astonishing.

A cosmic explosion is as unlikely to bring about life any more than a nuclear bomb would, unless it was engineered to do so.

Yet the conditions in our solar system and planet are perfectly attuned to creating life on earth.

---

[8]   R.E.D. Clark; Creation; 1946

Metaxas posed the questions: *"Can every one of those many parameters have been perfect by accident? At what point is it fair to admit that science suggests that we cannot be the result of random forces?"*

He reports the scientific odds against the universe existing are so astronomical that the notion that it all *"just happened" defies common sense.*

"It would be like tossing a coin and having it come up heads 10 quintillion times in a row," he claimed.

So, what exactly are the odds against human life existing from a random explosion in cosmic history?

A research article called *"Has Science Discovered God?"* on the Y-Jesus. com website, says the odds defy all the laws of probability.

The site, which operates as part of JesusOnline Ministries, makes some interesting analogies to help non-experts understand the odds.

"One astronomer calculates the odds at less than 1 chance in a trillion trillion trillion trillion trillion trillion trillion trillion trillion trillion trillion," the writer explains.

"It would be far easier for a blind-folded person - in one try - to discover one specially marked grain of sand out of all the beaches of the world."

It adds: *"Another example of how unlikely it would be for a random big bang to produce life is one person winning over a thousand consecutive mega-million dollar lotteries after purchasing only a single ticket for each."*

DNA - Nature's Computer Software

Astronomers are not the only scientists seeing evidence of design in the universe.

Molecular biologists, for example, have discovered that the coding in DNA is so sophisticated and intricate that it's the ultimate computer software programme.

In fact, Microsoft founder Bill Gates has famously been quoted saying that DNA is *"far, far more complex than any software we have ever developed."*

Inside the 37 trillion or so cells in every human body is DNA holding a code that is three billion letters long.

Genome expert, Francis Collins, has tried to explain the complexity of DNA code in a single cell:

"A live reading of that code at a rate of three letters per second would take thirty-one years, even if reading continued day and night." he wrote. [9]

The brilliance behind DNA coding can't be overstated. Science has discovered that 99.9% of DNA is similar to everyone's genetic makeup.

However, the sequencing is different in every single person.

It means that inside every cell in every person is a three-billion-lettered DNA structure that is unique to them.

Out of 7 billion people in the world today, no two will have the exact same DNA.

Molecular biologist and DNA's co-discoverer, Francis Crick, believed that the mini-computer within every cell could never have originated naturally.

"The origin of life appears at the moment to almost be a miracle, so many are the conditions which would have had to have been satisfied to get it going," he claims. [10]

Intelligent Design or Divine Creator

Still, most scientists continue to talk about 'intelligent design' rather than a Creator.

English physicist Paul Davies speaks of an unknown 'design' in the universe.

[9] Francis Collins; The Language of God; 2006
[10] Francis Crick; Life Itself; 1981

"There is for me powerful evidence that something is going on behind it all," he said. *"It seems as though somebody has fine-tuned nature's numbers to make the Universe…. The impression of design is overwhelming."* [11]1

Fred Hoyle, the astronomer who coined the dismissive term the "big bang," spoke about a 'super-intellect' behind the universe.

He argued that living organisms could not have arisen by chance alone.

"A junkyard contains all the bits and pieces of a Boeing 747, dismembered and in disarray," he writes. "A whirlwind happens to blow through the yard.

"What is the chance that after its passage a fully assembled 747, ready to fly, will be found standing there? So small as to be negligible…"[12]

Hoyles remarks were similar to Stephen Hawking's in A Brief History of Time:

"The remarkable fact is that the values of these numbers seem to have been very finely adjusted to make possible the development of life." [13]

Some scientists are determined to deny any possibility of a Divine Creator in the world.

Genome expert Crick preferred to attribute the genius behind DNA to aliens rather than consider a God.

In a theory called Directed Panspermia, he and British chemist Leslie Orgel suggested that life may have been started by an advanced extra-terrestrial civilisation.

Crick claimed that the universe is old enough for other intelligent civilisations to have built a spaceship and introduced organisms to the earth.

[11]   Paul Davies; The Cosmic Blueprint; 1988
[12]   Fred Hoyle; The Intelligent Universe; 1983
[13]   Stephen Hawking; A Brief History of Time; 1996

Not many scientists are convinced that the origins of the universe lie with aliens.

However, agnostic astronomer, physicist and cosmologist Robert Jastrow, acknowledged that many of his co-workers recoil from the idea of God.

"When a scientist writes about God, his colleagues assume he is either over the hill or going bonkers," he claimed.[14]

He also revealed some scientists' frustration that the possibility of a Creator can' be denied.

"For the scientist who has lived by his faith in the power of reason, the story ends like a bad dream," he wrote. *"He has scaled the mountains of ignorance; he is about to conquer the highest peak; as he pulls himself over the final rock, he is greeted by a band of theologians who have been sitting there for centuries."*[15]

A 2009 Pew Research Centre survey showed American scientists are half as likely as the general public to believe in God or a universal power.

Still, the survey also found that the percentage of scientists that believe in some form of a deity was 51 per cent.

One of those is U.S. geneticist Francis Collins, a former director of the Human Genome Project.

Collins, a convert from atheism to Christianity as a result of his work, sees a close affinity between God and new scientific discoveries.

"I have found there is a wonderful harmony in the complementary truths of science and faith," he wrote. [16]

"The God of the Bible is also the God of the genome. God can be found in the cathedral or in the laboratory. By investigating God's majestic and awesome creation, science can actually be a means of worship."

---

[14] Robert Jastrow; God and the Astronomers; 1978
[15] Ibid.
[16] Francis Collins; Why This Scientist Believes in God; CNN.com; April 6, 2007

Conclusion

Despite all the great scientific advances, there are many questions about the universe that science can't explain.

For the moment, the experts have more unanswered questions about how the world operates than they have answers.

There are many theories but no evidence to validate or give credence to any of them.

Yet for now, some people are remaining obstinately blinkered about the possibilities of a Creator.

I once read a simple analogy that helps us give us an insight into this way of thinking.

Imagine an explorer has landed on a desert island thousands of miles from anywhere.

Upon initial examination, it appears that mankind has never existed on the island at all.

Then the explorer sees something glitter in the sand, and as he approaches, he is astonished to see a watch.

He discovers that it is perfect working order, telling the seconds, minutes, hours and days.

There is no physical or visual evidence that any outside force is required for the operation of the watch.

There's no visible evidence that any outside force had anything to do with the creation of the watch.

Would it be logical, or could he reasonably conclude, that the watch assembled itself from the chaos of the universe, and started to operate all by itself?

In every area of scientific discovery, there is now more and more compelling evidence for the hand of God in Creation.

Yet inevitably you'll still hear that old chestnut: *"There's no such thing as God. It all started with the big bang."*

Science isn't even close to figuring out the origin of the universe.

But people assume science has sorted it all out.

This is where the saying "a little bit of knowledge is a dangerous thing" comes in.

The only ones who think science knows it all are people who know a little bit of scientific information and think they know a lot.

The experts are not so confident that they have it all figured out.

The most intelligent men and women on earth are still struggling to figure out the mysteries of this world with its breathtaking and incredible complexity.

And more and more of them are starting to believe that something far greater than we can conceive of has had a hand in its complex design.

A Psalm in Praise of God's Creation

"Lord, our Lord, how majestic is your name in all the earth! You have set your glory in the heavens… When I consider your heavens, the work of your fingers, the moon and the stars, which you have set in place, what is mankind that you are mindful of them, human beings that you care for them? You have made them a little lower than the angels and crowned them with glory and honour. You made them rulers over the works of your hands; you put everything under their feet: all flocks and herds, and the animals of the wild, the birds in the sky, and the fish in the sea, all that swim the paths of the seas. Lord, our Lord, how majestic is your name in all the earth!"

Psalm 8: 1-9

One Solitary Life

He was born in a stable, in an obscure village,
the child of a peasant woman.
He worked in a carpenter's shop until He was thirty.
From there He travelled less than 200 miles.

He never wrote a book. He never held an office.
He never had a family or owned a home.
He did none of the things one usually associates with greatness.

He became a nomadic preacher.
He was only thirty-three when the tide of popular opinion
turned against Him.
He was betrayed by a close friend, and His other friends ran away.
He was turned over to His enemies and went through the mockery of a trial.
He was unjustly condemned to death, crucified on a cross between two thieves
on a hill overlooking the town dump.
And, when he died, was laid in a borrowed grave,
through the pity of a friend.

Twenty centuries have come and gone,
all the armies that ever marched,
all the navies that ever sailed,
all the parliaments that ever sat
and all the kings that ever reigned,
have not affected the life of man on this earth
as that one solitary life.

An adaptation of a sermon by Dr James Allan Francis in "The Real Jesus and Other Sermons"
©1926 by the Judson Press of Philadelphia.

Author Biography

Father Sean Hyland was born in 1947 to Jack and Mary Hyland who raised their family on a small farm in Portarlington, County Laois.

He started his career with the ESB and trained in electrical engineering in Kevin Street College of Technology in Dublin.

He was employed as a commissioning engineer at a nuclear power installation in Ontario in Canada before marrying Liz Myron in 1972.

The couple had two children Seana and Kieran who both died while still in infancy.

In the 80s and 90s, Sean headed up manufacturing operations for international companies setting up in Ireland.

Controlling $100 million contracts, he spearheaded the start-ups of major American companies including Hewlett Packard.

He retired in 2006 and looked forward to travelling and playing golf with his wife.

However, Liz was diagnosed with cancer in April 2008 and died in December that year.

In 2009, in thanksgiving for many consolations of faith, Sean began exploring a vocation for the priesthood.

He started formation for the priesthood in the Pontifical Beda College in Rome in 2010.

He was awarded a Bachelor of Theology in 2013 and a graduate diploma in theology in 2014.

Sean was ordained a priest by Bishop Denis Nulty on July 13, 2014.

He lives in his hometown of Portarlington where he is a curate for the parishes of Rhode and Clonbullogue in County Offaly.